THE POETIC REPERCUSSION

Published By: Rings of Jupiter Publishing
                P.O. Box 841 | Atlanta, GA 30301
                www.ringsofjupiter.com

Library of Congress Cataloging-in-Publication-Data
Thomas, Mark Anthony
      [The Poetic Repercussion]
      The Poetic Repercussion: Mark Anthony Thomas
      ISBN- 0-9703649-1-1
      $9.95 (United States), $13.95 (Canada)

Cover Design and Book Layout: *Mark Anthony Thomas*
Cover Photography: *Jerrell Saddler (Cochran Mill Nature Park, GA)*
Printing Press Production: *King Printing Company, Inc.*
Content Consultants: *Sean L. Faulkner; Tiana J. Person; Harlan J. Porter; Tanya Spears; Tiffany Smith; Trenton Williams*
Project Consultants: *Chris Curtis; Howard Franklin; Gini Ikwuezunma; Anthony Keith, Jr.; Neusomba Long; Kisha Payton; Jerrell Saddler*
Works recorded, engineered, and remastered at locations in: *Athens, GA; Atlanta, GA; Dawsonville, GA; Henderson, NV; Houston, TX; Norcross, GA; New Orleans, LA; New York City, NY; Orlando, FL; Palo Alto, CA; Richmond, VA; St. Augustine, FL; Stone Mountain, GA; Tybee Island, GA; Washington D.C.;*

The following works have appeared and been featured elsewhere:
"Open Mic Nite" appears on spoken word CD, *Circle In The Way*, recorded at Island Exile Studio in Athens, GA.
"America to Redefine" written for Georgia State University 2002 Martin Luther King, Jr. Convocation
"So All People" written for the University of Georgia's 40th Anniversary Commemoration of Desegregation
"Handshakes Across The Globe" written for 2001 Athens International Festival
"I Too (Afraid I Am)" written for Women Against Domestic Violence, Inc.
"Heirs of Alpha" written for 2002 Metro Atlanta Alpha Phi Alpha Fraternity Founders Day Celebration
"Piece of Art" written for Georgia State University's 2000 International Photo Competition
"The Remission" written for the 2001 National Library Chain-Black History Month Read In

For More Information, visit: www.markanthonythomas.com

THE POETIC REPERCUSSION

Vol. II

Mark Anthony Thomas

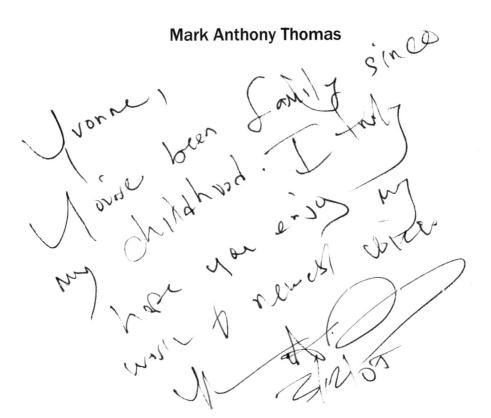

Yvonne,
You've been family since my childhood. I truly hope you enjoy my work & newest chapter.

"The thing that hath been, it is that which shall be;
and that which is done is that which shall be done:
and there is no new thing under the sun."

Ecclesiastes 1:9

ORDER OF APPEARANCE

< Prelude: Psychiatrist's Chair >

we
all walk down a-many roads
at congruent times—
 though no supernova,
 no paranormal
 powers

just human—
 with its complexities,
 triumphs & flights,
 with its vulnerabilities,
 deprivations & rights,

 with its fingerprints,
 irises & blues,
 with its imperfections,
 corrections
  —still subdued

& we've reached
the closing scene—
 the last act,
 the final leg,
 of a sore &
 battered mind

which brings me
here

< 1 >

THE WAKE

< by m.a.t. } instruments– Ecclesiasticus 13:17 >

1

i awoke from the chaos and the silence—
    the lack of symmetry in the dream;
i awoke from the cradle and the casket,
    and everything in between.

2

i awoke from the daybreak and the thunder—
    kissed the love and the solitude wrapped in the sheets;
mentally preparing for the ignorance and the awareness,
    the morning congestion on the streets.

3

i stretched to the sunlight and the asana—
    letting yarns signal sounds of the arrival;
i rose up towards the past and the future,
    over the continuance of the survival.

4

morning run through the desert and the forest—
    across the ghetto, across the seam;
i ran through the mystery and the evidence,
    and everything in between.

5

i showered in the deprivation and the blessings—
    writer's ink dried the purity and the filth;
mouth washed the free speech and the censorship,
    creative juices eased down the toothbrush's tilt.

6

i shampooed in the constraints and the courage—
    body lotioned the skin color unconsciously in;
i shaved off the normality and the hypocrisy,
    cutting the poetic barriers thin.

7

dressed with the pioneers and the followers—
    in helms of the delivered and the unredeemed;
i breakfasted the vitamins and the toxins,
    and everything in between.

8

ready for the adversity and the enjoyment—
    the interdependence and the places out-of-line;
left home for the defiance and the triumph,
    with the ecstatic and cadaveric entwined.

MIC CHECK

< by m.a.t. } instruments- Ecclesiastes 5:1 >

born, bathed, & bruised in grains of Gaia—
    it's hard to find someone to admire,
    let alone— grow to be wholly admirable;

in a world where humans are
fundamentally hypocritical

    but still find the audacity
    to make things they say

    sound as honest as tainted
    things they've said before.

I shake my head— knowing I was

shaped, sculpted, & subjected to teachings of Terra—
    to find someone to respect,
    & grow to be someone respectable
    (for others to vilify)

in a world where humans are not only
fundamentally judgmental

    but are crafted in apprehension,
    nurtured on condemnation then misconstrued
before they're even invited to speak;

yet— these are our kind of people

    people, we revere
    people, we follow
    people, we adore
    people, we groom

in the mirror— before we step
to the microphone

< 3 >

OPEN MIC NITE

< by m.a.t. } instruments- Job 16:5 >

the guys usually come
tight— but the women can use

that nite to vent on how men did
them wrong, how daddy was always gone
& how their heart now belongs

to the broken template of what love
should've been. but then again

when the jazz starts-a-playin'
& you're feelin' what the artists are saying

does it really matter what's being
said if the soul food being fed

can fill the appetite for strength & power?
& even those in their deepest hour—

can share their words with your mind & you'll
compare their words, to your words

to try to find a better way to free
the emotions you want to say—

in a more creative (yet mellow) way,
so when you embrace the mic on a future day,

the audience can see how you've advanced
to the next phase of your writing skills—

for you have to prove to yourself that you'll
stand & be respected for your literary expertise—

still relating to the "deep" at heart
while letting them know that a major part of
who you are
who you like to be
who they will now see as "me"
   is poetically
   intellectually
   theoretically incline.

< Interlude: Hand-Me Downs >

handed down… daddy's toleration,
   fitted for mama's cultivation;
years of lack of ventilation—

   made me a child of regulation;

handed down… TV's desecration,
   tailored for social adaptation;
measuring teen spirit depreciation—

   seeded for social alienation;

handed down… intellect fabrications,
    scriptures in jihad with temptations;
silenced on autonomy conversations—

   to avoid any poetic ramifications;

handed down…grandma's holy conviction,
   darkness fits light for opposition;
lesson planned a malediction—

   until I unlocked my declaration

< 4 >
DECLARATION
< by m.a.t. } instruments- 1 Corinthians12:8 >

under influence of influences,
persuaded by pressure of peer pressures,
   living life the fullest, their way,
and taking to heart what the proverbs say,

   quiet, I need your undivided attention,
   clear some space for my declaration.

viewing hindsight without 3-dimensional powers,
handling fate until Fate claims my final hours,
   learning how to do things, my way,
combating contradictions in what horoscopes say,

   can't be grown, thinking like childhood fools,
   while outlining my future under self-imposed rules.

gauging mercury heat under a self thermostat,
diffusing dark clouds holding sunbeams back,
   letting the breezes of wind blow relief my way,
and closing portals to what the witchdoctors say,

   the stage is ready, time for my feature presentation,
   while performing scripts of my proclamation.

shattering glass ceilings on my limits,
playing solitaire with tarot cards of psychics,
   interpreting destinies my own way,
and shielding ears to what the wise men say,

   once humbling myself under others' leadership,
   repurchasing all stocks under my ownership.

shooting for dreams with my ammunition,
compassing forest with my intuition,
   listening to echoes of harmony, my way,
before writing off reviews of what critics say,

   learning to maneuver gears for me to drive,
   and consciously follow my feelings inside.

'cause I'm a man now.

< 5 >

HIS LEFT HAND

< by m.a.t. } instruments– Judges 20:16 >

His left hand strings to
imagination in his vision;
irregularity connects to his passion—
poetic tears then flow.

they cry freedom;
they cry liberation;

His eyes gazed afar capture
vision in his imagination;
sights court dances with memory—
poetic imagery is retained.

they sling elation;
they sling illumination;

His insight then sorts among
concepts and pictures set aside;
visions find linkages with forms of dialect—
poetic thoughts are then born.

they disarm imagery;
they disarm tears;

gazed eyes are closed;
tears are wiped;

then Words are written.

<6>
FISHBOWL WITH WORDS

< by m.a.t. } instruments– Proverbs 25:9 >

Planning a night out
with Words is always difficult—

Consensus certainly beyond reach
with officious Predicates, introvert
Conjunctions, & the fickle Modifiers
who forever fail to remind me to bring

Cohesion when we finally
decide to head out—

Regardless— it's 11 p.m. Verbs are whispering
in ears of Pronouns, Adjectives appear
irritated, & Exclamations
sit at the kitchen bar consuming shots
of Etymology— all waiting on my collective

creative energy to assemble all parts of
an early adult culture & ideology to breath existence
into something tonight (for all of us to enjoy)

colossal task huh? but hey, here are my suggestions…

we got Taboo;
we got Spades;
we got DVDs;

Or we can always play Fishbowl?

(eyebrows heave—interests alert)

Oblivious to Fishbowl—Onomatopoeia asks for the rules:

1. Anonymously write a topic or question
2. Crumble & toss to the center
3. Then we pick, dissect & discuss
   until the ink runs out…
                    Cool?

Eyes hunt for harmony — then
Synonym & Allusion endorse
        (two of my closest confidants)

We congregate & the game starts—
   giving Words the chance:

To ration without speaking;
To query without questioning;
To inquire without outraging;

Sitting back & mostly observing—
   I'm really feeling this.

& Words who know it— Feel it too

< 7 >

LOVER TO THE ARTS

< by m.a.t. } instruments– Kings 3:12 >

I've always been
   the Lover to the Arts,

kissin' the lips
   embracin' the arms
of all her kinds;

once upon a time...

i wanted to paint
   with my inner voice
i wanted my inner voice
   to speak through the
artistry of painting
   moving
through the voices of
   Jacob Lawrence,
John T. Biggers,
   Hale Woodruff
that still resound today...

(more easily said) but
a young life began
    his renaissance with crayons
and blue-line paper sheets
    crafting dreams of sunbeam
filled skies and joys of days
    that only rays of sun could
replicate in the clarity of
    the voices we'd
paint together

    those were the days— until my voice
painted out of its range
    and sketched me out
of the portfolio
    of ability.

once upon a time...

i wanted to dance
    with my inner paintbrush
i wanted my inner paintbrush
    to move through
the rhythmic freedom of
    my body, in ways
the paintbrushes of
    George Snowden,
Leroy Jones
    grooved and still brush on today...

(more easily said) but
    my dreams found themselves
wrapping my body around the
    grove, passion of the pulses,
and the tenacity of the tempos.

    those were the days— until my paintbrush
missed a step
    and tumbled me outside
of the Lennox Lounge's side
    doors I once could slide through.

today...

i want to write
    with my inner cadence
I want my poetry

        to dance lyrics in
heartfelt performances
    like
Countee Cullen,
    Langston Hughes,
Zora Neale Hurston
    jazzed then and still dance on today...

 (more easily said) but
    my poetry finds itself floating
on the vibrato of the rhythm
    as words lock their experiences
into poetic fixations and give life to
    the songs
the dances
    the pictures
seen and touched by the
    renaissance of my young life

'cause there's this something special
    about how poetry tempts me as she
moves— and I've always been

the Lover to the Arts
    just-a kissin' and embracin'

< 8 >

FIREWORKS IN JUNE

< by m.a.t. } instruments- Ecclesiasticus 26:5 >

1
Sometimes I feel like Saturday's child,
   Waking to Monday's attitude;
Trapped in deserts with Africa's wild,
   Following the October full-moon.

2
Then days I dream like Tuesday's hopes,
   Until I stumble back on Wednesday's hump;
And fall down Canadian slopes,
   Watching sunlight in August slump—

\ but I'm not like this all the time \

3
I can easily wipe away Sunday's mourn,
   After feeling the joy of Friday's breeze;
Surviving off American bread and corn,
   Amazed at fireworks in June we receive?

4
Tired like commutes on Thursday's sunrises,
   Afraid like islanders after volcanic roars;
Atlantic tropics with hurricane surprises,
   Covered in snow at December's doors—

\ but I'm not like this all the time \

5
If seasons and days ever turn their tide,
   And permit Earth's quake to finally shake;
Unfastening screws for insecurities to collide,
   Allowing realities to differentiate.

6
Exposing fine print we've all tried to default,
   And repercussions we mirror & stare;
Correcting falsities before enemies aim to exalt,
   Hoping loose screws won't show through my hair—

\ but I'm not like this all the time \ I'm really not

< 9 >

1856

< by m.a.t. } instruments– Revelations 16:14 >

Character content-wise—
Lucifers are the largest minority;

never a formal proclamation of emancipation;
or amendment drafted to free them
to live as the citizens they've equally attuned to be—

no need to convene at railroads underground;
no written dialect to secretly learn & retain...

times have knocked at the doors of change
& we've extended the hand to welcome them in

to be assimilated, befriended, & subconsciously fully
submerged— while we imagine what it must be like

to be one of them;

at least I do— not in a left-handed Vodoun way;
but curious to know how it feels

to destroy lives; tear down senses of hope;
& crack the code behind the sorcery

we subliminally tap—
to merit & court the Wrath.

flour & cornmeal tile my floor;
lifeless black felines prowl at my front door.

Like those in this relentless pursuit of perfection—

it's my turn to be humanized & faceted
of the ideas of supernaturalism

& supremacy I've never chicken
boned the Loa to chase & claim;

obsolete now— black magical pins
are daggered at my name.

MISS CUPID-ITY

< by m.a.t. } instruments- Proverbs 31:29 >

With all I had to give— pride set aside;
    sorting through the fields of all the same;

This, and my heart, and all my feelings;
    found Miss Contradiction—
    who brought me games.

Do I magnet less than quality?
    do I draw the pictures
    of undesired?
Do I wear a sign within my soul that reads…
    "seeking a love that's
    worn and tired?"

Wherever flies her cupids may;
    wherever faults have
    wearied my chance;
Wherever lays my tries gone wrong
    smiles the broken
    arrow's trance;

Do I weaken my voice of reason?
    do the ides
    mystify my mind?
Do I wear a sign within my smile that reads…
    "seeking a love to
    charity my time?"

With all I had to give— reservations on hold
    eyes closed and it looks all the same;

This, and my heart, and my hopes for love;
    found Miss Cupid-ity—
    who brought me games.

< 11 >

PERFUME-FREE SCENTS

< by m.a.t. } instruments- Timothy 3:2 >

we tend to meet in
the most commoners' places;

places like harlem, chicago,
houston, atlanta, new orleans

cities lost within the black man—
which only you can conceive

as the woman who bears him;
as the bearer who comforts him;
as the comforter who strengthens him

as he defies the curse &
curses the defenders of injustice

but all is superlative.

we meet at contacts of eyes

in grocery stores, subway trains,
botanical gardens, coffee shops,

exchanging energies through your smiles,
affectionate hugs

& perfume-free scents

which I inhale and feel strong,
feel desired, feel received

by the black woman we fail to exalt;
by the un-exalted we fail to queen;
by the nubian queen we fail to tribute

as you draw courage through perseverance &
persevere to raise & elevate us to full manhood
          (single-handedly sometimes)

but all is superlative.

we celebrate your beauty

shown through your stance, your laughter,
your wool-like hair & the curves that shape you

all which I adore and come here to
acclaim, reverence, and bring vindication.

I find you in high corporate towers, education bases,
on concert stages, even as home-based blessings

in the most common & uncommon places

places like pensacola, boise,
muskegon, baton rouge, chapel hill

cities lost within the black man—
which only you can conceive

there to provide the love,
support, & strength I need

to make all superlative.

including this moment, including these words.

< 12 >

NATURAL BEAUTY

< by m.a.t. } instruments- 2 Samuel 11:2 >

You're a modern day renaissance
Overflowing with the creative juices
That bring deliverance to my spirit—
   Like a spiritual blessing

For only God could have created you

The Kings of Egypt,
The Roman Emperors,
The German Tyrants,

   Would all fall to your feet
   For your beauty transcends
   Years, decades, millenniums

For you have an ethereal appeal of endless allure

To love & worship you would become
Caesar's civic duty

For even Nostradamus couldn't
Foresee your modern & natural beauty

   No Marilyn,
   No Dorothy,
   No Madonna

But beauty, natural & pure,
Even the Modernist couldn't
Necessitate more

For inner beauty exists like
Grand Canyon-type amaze—
   Nothing unusual, just nature

Within its musical un-contrived ring—
   & everything else
   ranked as the next best thing.

< 13 >
EXACTLY WHY
< by m.a.t. } instruments- Matthew 22:6 >

You and i
are a balancing
act

as if we juggle the weight of our
work days with the relaxation
in our after-hours;

you toss me your mixed bags
of day long stresses / i hand
you my thorn filled flowers

/ the equilibrium conceives

but after the decks of cards fall
and our five speeds stall

it all leads to a good night kiss
exhaling after our
culminations hiss /

you collapse in my arms and I realize why,
exactly why...

Me and you
are a complimentary
two

as if our characters wrestle our traits
with the complexities and
depth of our conversations;

i toss you feedback on
what's on your mind / you hand me
critiques of my elaborations

/ then symmetry breeds

but after the bass drums prance /
and our passions dance

it all leads to fireworks inside
removing the silhouettes
of our pride /

i collapse in your arms and I realize why,
exactly why

< Interlude: Shoulder >

you
rub on
my shoulder
caress my neck
offer words & I push your hand— you look

in
surprise
& disbelief.
I shake my head, because you don't realize

you
have not
the slightest clue
but think that by you rubbing my shoulder

&
gently
caressing my
neck and offering words it is the best

you
can do
when it is so
much deeper than just love—to make this work.

< 14 >
OCEAN TIDES

< by m.a.t. } instruments– Ecclesiasticus 25:23 >

Her moods—
real bad moods

pull All of Earth
under distress— yet

she introduces me
— as being from
Mars when

I grow from Earth—
too

Her legs touch my
hands— Her

neck kisses my
lips— Her

breasts stimulate
my tongue

to shoot for my
excitement but

misses completely /

Her tears—
Irritation filled tears

drought All of Earth's
oceans— yet

she introduces me
— as being from
land when

I'm salt water dependent—
too

Her hair runs through
my fingers— Her

hips churn in my
center— Her

back shivers
around my tongue

to shoot for my
arousal but—

she finds her Mars'
man needing Earth

to grow— and finds
Her land creature

In need of sea water.

< 15 >
BRIDGE BETWEEN VERSES

< by m.a.t. } instruments– Ecclesiastes 8:6 >

ahh   mission established
disappointment is my lighter fluid
frustration   is my reasoning

isolation   is my chauffeur
empty is my understanding—

(refrain): kind of late in this game
    no heart or pride to defame
    and no hit man to perform task for me—
    because you're unaware
    that your heart's not where
    I wish its focus would be /

trust isn't   my companion
overjoyed is no where to be found

indecisive   is my status
foundation is my purpose's ground—

no surprise   love is the vehicle,
and too fast is the speed we ride,

pointing fingers   is the method,
to release the hurt held inside—

(refrain): giving up kind of quick,
    no doubt need be shown
    for burning love's bridge between you and me—
    because you're unaware
    that my heart's not where
    its connectivity should be /

then mission   completed.

shivering   were all my fingers
feeble was strongest source of fire

slow was the flame to destroy us
all burned   except our hearts' desire—

for internal hurt felt in the mission
and closed were my eyes at the impact

young was my expertise for task
and no outcry or commotion could distract.

mission evaluated—

doubt now falls like the tears of silence
as the cars bringing your reflections burned too
but the casualty was my quest for love
a love I might be losing in you.

< 16 >

TEARS HOLDING ON

< by m.a.t. } instruments- Psalms 22:14 >

you don't even have to say it / my heart reads
  your thoughts / my tears are trying to
not fall / with the future of our failed
  attempt to make this love work /

for my eyes tremble with the fear &
  hesitation my tongue endures / as you
watch my words prevent themselves /
  from rolling out of my mind

knocking your emotions over / like bowling pins
  sending tears down the alley of a failed love's
repercussions / my heart knows what
  your mind feels / but my body feels the

ache of the frail skeletal framework of a love
  that insufficiently formed / for we both know it
began to starve & hunger for more / &
like anything famished / no need to beg /

no need for words / we could see the hunger
  one can sense the negligence / we could feel the chills
& even the pain / & my heart doesn't want
  to handle the strain / when it's hard enough for me to

maintain a straight face at this time / knowing &
  feeling my tears holding on one by one / to the
small hope within my mind / that I have to decline
  from this love we share / though we're not ready to bear

having our emotions knocked over like bowling pins / sending
  tears down the alley / of a failed love's repercussions

…making tears fall like water trickling off icicles /
  once I shine light on the realization
that our relationship grew cold / froze & now must
  dissolve in the heat of reality.

< 17 >
PACKING 4 COLLEGE

< by m.a.t. } instruments– Daniel 1:4 >

leave that barrel of baggage in the basement,
    leave that dais of diffidence in your room;
leave that pack of purity under the bed—
    & don't come home anytime too soon.

leave parental sanction in the disposal,
    leave that unorganized faith & trust unsaid;
leave that voided reality check unpaid—
    & don't come home secularly fed.

keep that significant other at distance,
    keep self-skeletons taped on your closet door;
keep the strobe light aglow at deficiencies—
    & let the lava lamp spring up more.

take a little cockiness 4 the dorm room,
    take along the stretcher 4 the tendencies;
take the piggy bank to stash all the changes—
    & don't come home 'til you're at your knees.

< 18 >
SO ALL PEOPLE

< by m.a.t. } instruments– For Charlayne Hunter; Hamilton Holmes >

Together they embarked the journey,
Encountering widespread agitation—
    But they withstood the pain,
    So All People could equally obtain;
Georgia's flagship in education.

In the midst of civil turmoil,
Divinity deemed 1961 as their moment to shine—
    No college memories of festivity,
    So All People could proudly see;
Diversity welcomed in their lifetime.

Days attached to discomfort & strife,
Called them to be composed & courageous—
    A story that should never lay unstated,
    So All People would've appreciated;
The Arch's seal in their memoir's pages.

Spearheading decades of black excellence,
From the Southland to Georgia's varsity—
    Pioneering a passage for reception,
    So All People could sing less opposition;
Georgia—hail to thee!

< Interlude: Saturday School >

Fight songs awake me. Window view
shows villages of RVs and

tailgaters. We Forget
it's only football. I see children

dance in university colors. They
know nothing about college—

but it begins here. People unify without
conflict. Charcoal smoke mingles

with the pieces of heaven (where
have I been). We Forget

it's only football. Three hours until
kick off. Unlit kegs & under-grilled

hotdogs could never tell. It's easy to
find a friend. Guess this thing

will take us there (wherever
there is). We Forget

it's only football.

GAME DAYS 101

< by m.a.t. } instruments– 2 King 10:3 >

it's Game Day— but the
"do not disturb" sign has been
removed— the bell rings

Football—
Patient, Analytical
Intensifying, Hastening, Tackling
Gold-Chain-Fields, Downward-Touch—Hole-In-One, Hole-High
Relaxing, Politicking, Conversing
Exclusive, Upscale
Golf

Basketball—
Energetic, Intricate
Challenging, Urban-Centering, High-Flying
Throws-for-Free, Three-Finger-Pointers—Run-Home, Slam-Grand
Yielding, Past-Timing, Enduring
Customary, All-American
Baseball

Hockey—
Fast-Pace, Aggressive
Antagonizing, Frostbiting, Clawing
Lined-Blue, Circle-Faced—Goal-kept, Eminent
Winging, Foot-Dribbling, Mounting
Strong-Legged, Intercontinental
Soccer

"do not disturb" sign
has been reinstated. Why?
It is still Game Day.

< 20 >

HOOD COCOONS

< by m.a.t. } instruments– Matthew 25:15 >

Money for school nonexistent— Unless I can seize
a ball & craft the magic wand-type startle to lure
higher eds to cocoon me within athletic rosters &
transform my wings into collegiate colors—

    While shaking hand— &
    offering to fuse in an
      education too.

Many hoops & free throws away— But when
This young Startler from the hood looks at the Dream
From Hampton, Virginia— Who went on to be Allen Iverson—
Can't help but smile knowing I could too follow his
make come true.

The End Goal finds Itself fitting uniforms for
baseball little league teams— Knowing a Donora,
Pennsylvanian transformed into Ken Griffey, Jr.
Home runs & strike outs away— The Goal can't help
but to float—

    Inside the batter's
    mind— As he prepares for the
      life transformation.

The Boys & Girls Club tackles Drive in after-
school football practices— But He'll rise to, like the
Drive from Folkston, Georgia— Knowing after the
winning touchdowns & field-goals— He too can
grow to be a Champ Bailey.

Today I still pillar on grounds— While learning
to master the making of that something of silk-like
splendor— Money for school nonexistent—

    Starting here with a
    dream— looking for my only
      chance to fly away.

ON A DEFEAT

< by m.a.t. } instruments- Proverbs 15:13 >

so we meet again—
   lost without failure
disappointment but not defeat
   although second place comes home empty handed

I'm full of enough pride,
   enough competitive glory;
to let any lost, any defeat,
   put a damper on my story.

yet, it's nothing like not hearing your name called,
     and watching your victory
       carried away
         by someone else—
         only to be
      left
              with the supporters'
    sympathy and
   a question of
  misunderstanding
 within one's self.

so we meet again— to reflect
   on a lost, without the rules of a test;
on a defeat, within a race of winners
   although my forecast superior to the rest;

handed my share of bewildered looks,
   my sighs breathe thoughts, "I gave my best,"
apologetic howls refrain,
   their poise far too proud to unrest.

yet, it's nothing like giving my all,
     and watching the final score come too
      short to give way—
        only to be
      left
with an outer silence, and
    absence of
     sportsmanship
      I can't
      portray.

< 22 >

PIECE OF ART

< by m.a.t. } instruments- Acts 2:17 >

Take a picture of failure—

I'll show a piece of art called victory;
    for no image of failure is permanent
Close your eyes and you'll begin to see—

The image of the void only you can fill;
    the journey that's so far away
So pack your bags to start the hike up the hill—

To the castle of dreams & hidden room of hope;
    if you find no direct stairway
Search for the window to cast a rope—

To climb through the opportunities on the side;
    using strength and spiritual provision
To pull your inner motivation and pride—

To climb to reach that window of chance;
    to feel and hold the bright future
Within the strength of your shivering hands—

You'll then view your future— with room for no regret;
    As you re-open your eyes
To see remnants of dreams you set—

And as time passes— make each dream come true;
    For the piece of art is your allegiance
And you'll see our eyes glowing at you.

NEW CHILDREN OF FLOWERS

< by m.a.t. } instruments– Deuteronomy 13:6 >

so u read one philosophical book
  and now u're a militant?

u had one deep revelation
    and u're a revolutionist?

    what a joke.

oh mother, center ur daughter
    so she'll have completeness in tact;
oh father, educate ur son
    so he can separate theory from fact

and when they're dropped in the
    melting pot of philosophy;
they won't link to the first group
    offering them community.

u went to one communal rally
  and u've converted ur convictions?

u tasted one indulgence
  and it changed ur perceptions?

    come again?

oh mother, read to ur daughter
    so she won't live a contradiction;
oh father, navigate ur son
    so culture won't fog his premonition

and when they're left in the
    center of intellectual birth;
they won't breed new children
    of flowers on earth.

believe me or not / this is my only life—
prophets find God's favor in it / ancestors find their future in it;

enemies find faults where they can /
single women find a ring-fitting hand;

       & you reach for my soul only to touch human flesh
living life from the script / nothing more, nothing less

       / then i tap dance until my feet ache
until my disenchanted thoughts congregate.

i'm convinced i'll only get one life / whether or not—
all adversaries agree with it / lonely hearts can live with it;

generations see my purpose at hand /
angelic causes find a pad to land;

       & you taste of my youth only to savor human skin—
setup for predeterminations / disinclined to bend

       / then i perform my songs without the jazz
though my unseen strings are the show's pizzazz

< 24 >
ACCEPTANCE SPEECH
< by m.a.t. } instruments– Isaiah 5:21 >

I am meaningless—

   addict for attention;
poster boy for credibility;
   huntsman for exaltation—

Living off you—

   cause my merit & acceptance by
the beautiful people we see welcomed
   by media & the initiates of conformity symbols—

mean I mean something...

as I reinvent my
    existence to be celebrated as

the immortal case of triumph
    you should praise me for

continuing to be.

(Intermezzo:
    The presenter calls my name—crowds applaud

  Acceptance Speech:
    "This is all new to me—
    I feel beautiful & finally feel right—
    This is larger than my ordinary life")

tabloid my own tattletales—
revolve my own rumors; but

Worth from you—

decorate my walls, resume
    paper, & merit

with certificates that gratify
    my search for any derivative of
reception— allocate

my time & energy to entertain
    you, those pretty people,
& the military of judgers

who will hunt & slay my poster boyhood,
    attention addiction, & crisis my
false sense of identity

    when I'll realize I am meaningless...

& aspire to change—

just not 'til after
I collapse on stage.

< 25 >

SEASON PASS

< by m.a.t. } instrument – 2 Samuel 22:6 >

It took me two crutches
hopping inside the
theme park of turmoil—

during a Season in Hell
to realize: Things had to change;

it wasn't those crutches I despised—
no bloody cry aloud or unbowed head
could justify how—

an 18-year old boy could fit perfectly
inside the mask of the Great Liar—

while surrendering his pride to pledge
the seasonal fare for admission
before: Things had to change;

I wanted it so badly—

so good intentions permitted
sending uncanny beast-like strikes
& Emotional blows

to the point I'd accidentally
two-face injury— with one face wearing
the mask of the Great Liar—
& the other towards the

Surgeon to hand me crutches
in recovery to become a man with
soles of wind & strut across a runway
of External disguises.

But I fell—
                    fell down
              years of an
          Internal
Contradiction—

only to rise & shake hands
with thousands of Milligrams

of Painkillers to Ferris Wheel
the damage— though it only spun toward
feelings of Worthlessness

'Cause the costs were too high for
what I took home in return. &
as I relearned who I remained—

I knew: Things had to change;

Roller Coasters laughed at
    my compliance; Merry-Go-Rounded
me with humiliation;

Clowns awarded tickets when
    the Public Amusement toppled
Shame & spectators cheered offering

celebration-style balloon drops for me
to rejoice in— while my injured leg
jeered without jokes

As tickets swelled & equaled prizes of—
    Permanent damage,
    Twisters of cover ups,

Then Medals of Service camouflaged
a Season in Hell's Certificate of Failure—

leaving a Damned soul to rise from
the black Pit with flames I'd commit
to uphold too— which is why

I knew: Things had to change;

Just at my expense.

< 26 >

♩42♩

GRADUATION HORS D'OEUVRES

< by m.a.t. } instruments- Luke 8:14 >

Brochures 4 college flocked mama's
mail.   No stories they forgot
                    Not to tell of

                    No classes
I can't fail   No experiments
    I can dry spell   No esteems
I can't convince   No militants
    I can't commence   No drugs

I can't try   No underage drinks
    I can't buy   No fears
I can't hold onto   No girls
                        (who'll groin me blue)

Brochures 4 college flooded mama's
mail.   No stories they forgot
                    Not to tell of

                    No intramurals
I can't toy   No purities
    I can't destroy   No color blinds

I can't counterpoint   No flexibility
    I can't un-joint   No devils
I can't maintain   No asana

I can't attain   No falsetto
    I can't front   No betrayals
I can't confront   No misfortunes

I can't avoid   No substitute
    I can't out-void   No revelation
I can't wing, with   No confrontation
                    (with what college brings)

Flocked in masses in mama's
mail.   What they didn't forget
                    not to tell.

< 27 >

SITTING GROWN (A Fugue)

< by m.a.t. } instruments- 1 Corinthians 3:8 >

the confusions I know,
   the problems they sow;
the drive intrinsically,
   and what it says to me—

the successes I stare;
   the blindfold I wear,
the career I can not see,
   and what it all says to me—

(refrain):
   sitting grown—
     sitting figuring
out what to be?

   sitting unfound
     on un-solid ground
   crafting a future I can not see?

the style my talents brand,
   holding fast to dreams at hand;
the individuality I free,
   and what it says to me—

the hopes to make come true,
   the drive to pull them through;
the sacrifice I would have to see,
   and what it all says to me—

(refrain)
   sitting grown—
     sitting puzzled
on a profession I can not quite name?

   hoping if you would
     ask me tomorrow,
my thoughts would not be the same

< 28 >

BLACK MAN'S WORK

< by m.a.t. } instruments- Job 40:18 >

it's 5:30 a.m.

got my father's name to better,
got recession's storm to weather,
got my black women to queen,
got affirmative's actions to clean,

got ignorance to un-label,
got calamities to un-table,
got my families to un-break,
got confirmations to un-make,

why must I have to prove, all I said I can do?
why must I fight to be, all I said I can be?

got athletics to un-typecast,
got spiritual gardens to un-fast,
got inferiority's terms to un-instill,
got prison's cells to un-fill,

got video cameras on observe,
got statistics fighting to un-curve,
got inequalities to un-endure,
got predictions of failure to un-secure,

why must I confirm, all I said I could learn?
why must I show to be, all I said I could be?

as a black man— that's the reality
before my workday
even begins

it's 6 a.m.

< Interlude: Downtown >

Here they all move—Street Vendors, Judged, Corner
Preachers, & Panhandlers fumbling
beneath high-rises of power
to impulse & entice the
sympathetic at heart
to invest, even
nest their feelings
of always
being
less.

< 29 >

CUBICLE SOLILOQUY

< by m.a.t. } instruments– James 5:4 >

"they leave me fully
walked over— jacket

thrown down first—
feet upon my head

& left to flutter in
the wind— barely speak

for I'm just the
wind-fluttered-puddle

of mud— insignificant &
irrelevant, at best. out of the

case where my talent is
needed less," he said.

(nobody nods their head)

"on the american grounds
& glass ceilings controlled

by corporate culture— I've
signed my life to be a

defender of the curse &
a subsidiary of the slanted

system— without validation
of formal degrees &

specialties, by no means
will I taste my slice

of American's dessert—
at least here," he said.

(nobody responds)

"never feeling so empty
before— watching the little

value I have shatter at the
doors closed at my face

where my little skill & value
added have no place—

for I am just dust
of the earth— trivial at best,

with more than my divvied up
shares of stocks toward

feeling less— then they utter words
to me— condescendingly," he said.

(nobody's there to listen)

< Bonus Track >

'Fraid So

young man—

if you've cleaned
the floors I den cleaned—
you're no co-worker,
you the clean-up crew.

If you've scrubbed
the windows I den scrubbed—
you ain't goin' to no company picnic
you clean up after it.

I sweep what falls upon the ground—
even my pride.

If you've emptied
the garbage cans I den emptied—
you're no colleague.
you're fired...

if you forget to clean one floor,
scrub one window,
or empty out one of those garbage cans.

Then you carry the weight of
superior remarks;
igniting rages of sparks, 'cause

I empty what's tossed into the trash—
even my purpose.

when, last time I remember—

I got a family like de do.
I cry tears like de do.
I shed esteem like de do.
& gotta life to live, like de do too.

Is respect too much
to ask for too?

'fraid so.

< 30 >

IN THIS SHOP

< by m.a.t. } instruments– Ezekiel 5:1 >

status means nothing

and it falls voluntarily like
the hair to the
ground— least it should

in this shop— the barber shop

where we can share
unrestrained   uncontained
thoughts

without being judged
convicted and
tagged confused— in a nation so quick too

i grow here

i realize my place   & connect in a
familiar space   while shaving my face
of the blue eyes and blond hair

any of my successes could indict me of being.

and in this place—
which celebrates the luxuries
of being what we are

not what happened
to us   not how the media
portrays us   not the fathers
who fathered us

but   what we aspire us to be
and how little things, done subconsciously

like conversation
like connectivity
like consolation

and a haircut— could mean so much.

< 31 >
WARRANT A SEARCH
< by m.a.t. } instruments– Romans 14:13 >

Men are taught that they will idolize
Athletes, War Heroes, CEOs
and all that's lateral.

so they hide behind safeguarded associates
to not warrant a search
through their boxes of G.I. Joes and Legos
to find anything of remote creativeness

Men are told to be
Dominant, Athletic, Competitive,
and all that's tangential.

so they hide behind crudeness
to not warrant a search
through their collection of baseball cards
to find anything artistic;

The forefathers set the track
for even the most God-like man to have
points tapped off his back
if he rebels when

Men are told to love by
Shepherding, Womanizing, Authorizing,
and nothing contrary.

so they hide behind senses of apathy
to not warrant a search
through their stash of condoms and pornographic
materials to find their heart's vulnerability;

Men are supplied tools to be
Fraternal, Aggressive, Nebulous,
but nothing sensitive.

so they hide behind chauvinism and phobias
to not warrant a search
through their athletic equipment and tool drawers,
to find keys to unopened doors—

unless their manhood is secure.

< 32 >

CAR GEOMETRY

< by m.a.t. } instruments- 1 Corinthians 3:10 >

man— that
I am. but you

have never
been a favorite subject—

besides changing
oil— tires— out-blown

fuses— you
know I know nothing—

even after
reasoning— & engine code

interpretations reach
toward my wallet— to

defend negative
dives— into my accessible

funds— to
make me a cheerful

commuter again—
along this line of

reliance— alone
I am with indecisive

instinct— suspicious
intuitions & this dysfunctional

vehicle— now
solely dependent on a

car quotient—
I can not gauge.

< 33 >

LOOKING TOWARDS FOOTPRINTS

< by m.a.t. } instruments- Ecclesiastes 3:1 >

Faster than vehicles on cruise control,
Carrying time at the speed of a passenger's hold;
To a wheel of life he has no control,
Looking at how
        quickly his story is told.

Questions of "how fast" sink into reflections' beat,
As phases zoom with no hold to repeat;
In a life slowly dying at every heart's beat,
Looking towards footprints
        before he moves his feet.

When sets of footprints no longer fit his size,
And time ticks, as seasons recur so wise;
Then years contract into understanding's size,
Looking at how life
        slips by before his eyes.

Knowing life's crossroads will light after he'll pass,
From the glow of sand in God's hourglass;
Measuring salvation in good works that amass,
Looking for entry in
        the eternal upper-class.

< Interlude: Radio Frequency >

i-85 south; radio on—

"into having sex I ain't into making love…"
        (click)
 "I bet you want the goodies- bet you thought…"
        (click)
"gonna have you naked by the end of this song…"
        (click)
"it's gettin' hot in herre, so take off all your clothes…"
        (click)
"it's like murder she wrote, once I get you out them clothes…"
        (click)
"I got the magic stick, I know if I can hit once I can hit twice…"
        (click)

no wonder.

< 34 >

CROSSOVER HIGHWAYS

< by m.a.t. } instruments- Luke 12:52 >

Son— I'm talking about real music here

when hip hop was more than
the vehicle to flash jewelry

to showcase cribs
to spin wheels around
vehicles that eclipse the cost of
the houses we don't own

but when it actually meant something—

I'm talking about hip hop
before hip hop became pop.
in fact— hip hop owes us an apology

for paving streets like...
illmatic
reasonable doubt
all eyez on me
ready to die
the low end of the theory

then redistricting so crossover highways
could cut right through the hearts of our hoods...

roads where mainstream access
has gradually increased

for once-restricted vehicles to
chart radio-friendly hits

taking away the one unifying medium
that we could call our own

and hey ya— maybe I'm seeing this wrong...

that the soundtrack of our lives is a hit in
the pop culture theaters—

such a success, that they now pack the seats
request after request, video after video
track after track

and help control and profit from
the vehicle to debase our women
to glorify our poverty
to even exalt pimping

vehicles that eclipse the cost of
the educations they fail
to realize we can't afford

and hey ya— maybe it's just me that's not on board.

< 35 >
CROSS DRESSING
< by m.a.t. } instruments– Numbers 35:3 >

from the porch of my
suburban home I have watched

hip-hop

once distanced at sight—
now strolling along the lines

of what defined and confines
white culture security—

straddling the likes of
p. diddy, outkast, and jay-z—

bedroom walls unfolding scrolls
that deem tupac and notorious b.i.g.

as the icons of the new
allegiance my children

have pledged to—

right hand on heart—
ott my sons and daughters go

cross dressing in the street culture
from head to toe

STREET RUMORS

< by m.a.t. } instruments- For Hip Hop >

Born as Hip Hop— People have assigned
    Nicknames to classify who they think I
Should be— & for defined periods of
    American cultured times— I accordingly adjusted &

Fully embraced— while grasping onto the classification
    & welcoming who I thought I should
Be for them. Still— I'd rejoice in
    All sounds (if not fancy). Since my

Initiation— all collaborations with musical links remained
    Constrained & guarded to ensure the genres
I connected with— didn't negatively reflect the
    Collective conformity—

Then the need was felt to expand
    & open minds to notarize signatures of
Innovation for even my most conventional artistic
    Moments (years past the backing and validation
from the most critical of the critics)—

    If only success was so one-dimensional;

Still unaware of the image I was
    Constrained to remain— Gospel secretly disguised a
Meeting with Pop, Blues, & Rock to
    Address & discuss circulating street rumors alleging

That I had integrated elements of American
    Cultured times that would attract backlash &
Condemnation by the audiences they aim to
    Appease. Having recently confronted some artistic
distances—

Pop no longer my roommate, Blues marrying
    Jazz, Rock living out of state, &
Gospel reminding me of my connections it
    Could benefit from— Outside of occasional MC

Battles & edgy stage performances— I've never
    Been one to celebrate in triviality or
Engage in actions jeopardizing the crosses I
    Wear across testimonies embezzled in lyrics that

Represent how I subsist. What an awful
    Evening— with artists & albums highlighted for
Explanations to be called upon. Looking &
    Defending in disbelief that the medium binding

Us became an unabridged forum for confrontation
    On a brand I can't honestly own—

    If only life was so one-dimensional;

But types are— Especially those who have
    Become genres looking for this prime occasion
To springboard my condensation— Vulnerable, I share
    Stories— Reveal revolutions for which I fight—

Even divulge secrets my pioneers asked me
    To never share. Only to be greeted
With close-mindedness & contradictory efforts to regard
    My accounts— No longer can I reach

Out to sounds who've cornered & assaulted
    My inclusion of elements of American cultured
Times that have created false reports of
    An injuriousness I don't represent or sustain.

    If only music was so one-dimensional;

My nicknames die. My accessibilities restrict. My
    Roots find distance. Born as Hip Hop— &
Finally learning who I will have to
    Be— To rejoice in my own sound
(If not fancy).

< 37 >

GOD TRENDY

< by m.a.t. } instruments– Exodus 23:1 >

God is no trend—

He's no artistic statement
we tattoo into our skin;

No relic linked to party
chain jewelry around our necks;

Nor nested in song lyrics
written for the barn hay He
permits us to light & smoke

(cough, cough)

God is no superstar—

He's no theme choreographed
with dancers on Broadway to;

No receiver of props we
give before the producers
& video directors;

Nor characters we craft in
cinematic parodies

(next joke)

God is no secularist—

He is no vain we damn His
name with under excitement;

No name we scream & oh for
at midnight climactic peaks;

Nor the positive note we
end musical albums of
radio friendly pop hits

(next song)

< 38 >
TO EVOLUTION

< by m.a.t. } instruments–Job 26:7 >

though your every move is important—
     forward thinking is the
pinnacle attribute;

you move forward, analyze,
     find comfort, & transcend
so amazingly, so deviously;

fooling & confusing your own
     expanded viewpoints to think you were
once narrower in your yesteryears.

we chuckle at your theorists;
     we find hilarity in
your followers' convictions—

who welcome you; interpret you;
     as their predictions   resort to
sand grains to craft your next steps—

gauging from your yesterways.
     & while others laugh at you—
while you gather & pack all of

your things— we become children
     reaching to be held in your arms
"carry me with you"

for change is the stranger
     of mankind   & you are clearly
our most beautiful stranger

enticing us to dance even closer & taste of
     your knowledge so we can also leave our
yesterhaviors behind.

smiling— with your sly, clever grin—
     saving your mysterious plans within
for no duration can define you;

only God's word undermines you.

< 39 >

DIVINE SENSE

< by m.a.t. } instruments– Malachi 2:10 >

organized religion
is what divides

us— & easily overlooks
that we are

all born sinners &
must all be saved.

but we're dissecting
souls here— not

any skin they're in— not
flesh & frames

that serve as prey to
The enemy's trickery— not

the lust of lust or
opened spaces for

the Cross of tattoo
markings & piercings—

that the organized
system that

divides us easily
condemns (again, we're

by no means—
the anti-Christ or

against Trinities)
but we preach

to the Channels
crafted in prehistoric

homosapien times— to
assemble us under

doctrines— &

construe aggregate

guidelines to defy the
calls of nature &

purify our tainted
from birth

cores. &
on paper it all

makes divine sense—
in 34,000 Organized

ways. redefining,
reassuring, dividing,

& easily forgetting
that we are

all born sinners &
must all be saved.

INTERMISSION SHOW

< by m.a.t. } instruments- Proverbs 22:6 >

Mama's eyes said, "you bet not show
out in church today!" Last

Sunday I did fallout a few
times— erupt in erratic tears— &

slide along the pews— redirecting
the congregation's attention

from Him to here.

the usher carried me out—
Mama followed suit & stumbled

onto Sister Joyce's two-week
old switch to knock my behavioral

malfunction back into place. didn't
stop me from falling back out &

dropping off a few tears again to
redirect the congregation's limelight

from Him to here.

First lady tried to ignore— Reverend
avoided commentary— but the church

mothers' unspoken stares made it obvious
it was my time for training in

the way I needed to go.   Not like
I didn't intuitively know— just

wanted to act up an intermission show
& pull the congregation's focal point

from Him to here.

< 41 >

RESET IN THIRD PERSON

< by m.a.t. } instruments- Psalms 30:7 >

Set 893 miles from his birthplace— nothing
metaphorical, but the physical
ground that staged his entry into
this temporary world—

he rocks on the porch
looking towards new worlds— while
the home behind him crumbles

day-long bicycle journeys, amusement
park rides with cousins, video games &
street basketball

descend to memories— instead
of companions along the paths
of present footprints, as

exterior forces overhaul
& dictate his priorities reset in third person.

(then his uncles remind him how
 long it's been since he's come to visit)

as he opens the screen door
to greet new opportunities— while
the roots behind him meet blockage.

unrehearsed family gathering, late-night
movie rentals, barbeques & after-church
Sunday dinners

descend to afterthoughts— instead
of company along the forethoughts
continuously shaped, as

outside influences surmount
& direct his focuses reset in third person.

(then his aunts remind him of
 the mortality of his ancestors)

and he looks back.

< Interlude: Cycle >

times are hard,
but don't let
    your spirit be;
trust is here,
but don't let
    your departure be;
mercy is soft,
but don't let
    your endurance be,
money is short,
but don't let
    your patience be;
children are plentiful,
but don't let
    your worries be;
bills are late,
but don't let
    your cycle be:

        'cause the last thing we need,
        is another mouth to feed

        'cause the last thing our ship can afford,
        is another passenger aboard

continuing the cycle

< 42 >

CHILD SUPPORT CHECKMARKS

< by m.a.t. } instruments- Colossians 3:21 >

those child support checks were the
    only reminder of you we had—
and they stopped coming when I turned six.

but unfortunately

I had your sinful eyes *(check)*
    your mellow complexion *(check)*
    your deceptive smile *(check)*
&   your narrow mind *(check)*

    and I continued to remind mama of

    your departure,
    your exit, and
    your stoic demeanor towards our survival—

and the support you never sent,
made my life's existence an accident,
and the support she didn't see,

was debited from the
support given to me *(check)*

< 43 >

ALL OVER

< by m.a.t. } instruments– Ecclesiastes 4:9 >

Sunrays peek from
the one-hundred and three
degrees angle to pierce skin like
pores— humidity takes
center stage while
Artic

winds sleep until
November— giving room
for the heat on urban summers
to gently massage all
over body parts
of the

subtropical
Earth we call home— And the
love you feel; All over. Over
your hands— over thoughts of
entrapment. All
over.

Over years of
no where to go- but hoop-
less apartment basketball courts
(which watch over preteen
black boys who seek
outlets

from alluring
street temptations). 'Til the
old school bells ring for red kool-aid
and the Candy Lady's
sweet lemonade—
But we

choose to indulge
in the ice-cream man's range
(fifty cents out of change); though no
lost; no pain— 'cause you feel
the love. Whether
yo friend's

Ma fries chicken
for you, the neighbor's boy
and the new Hispanic boy from
down the street— Re-watching
Disorderly,
The Last

Dragon, Crush Grove
And Beat Street— But Mortal
Kombat, Street Fighter II, even
Double Dribble give much
fun— Comfort for
black boys

who all won't see
the age of twenty-one.
So we come together in ways
Coca Cola TV
commercials, the
Artists

for Africa,
and British icons, would
nod their heads in approval— for
even they can feel the
love (and you would
too). Feel

it all over—
over your hands— over
thoughts of inadequacy; but
consciousness comes in with
time maturity—
stretching

lenses beyond
candy-ladies, hoop-less
rims, and teenage fitted caskets,
toward prevalent thoughts
of confinements—
concealed

in plain view of
inferiority—
rained with widespread complacency.

PRODUCT OF DIVORCE

< by m.a.t. } instruments- Ephesians 6:4 >

like every Earth-born man,
just wanting a father to lead your childhood home;
but—like any product of divorce,
father figurate confined to a telephone.

like any man under God,
just wanting a father to lead you in prayer;
but—like any product of divorce,
bowed for grace with the image of Adam not there.

(chorus)   /   learning to tie
                 your own tie,
                 the man of the house
                 adult years shy.

growing up redirected through divorce;
compensated by garnished wages from the court;
lessons on manhood are where you came up short;
& lacked the full circle of un-levied child support.

no memory of an in-house father loving his wife;
& distant hands molding an incomplete life;
no in-house father reflecting a spiritual light,
as the product of divorce left to fill void's price.

(chorus)   /   struggling to tie your tie,
                 man of the house
                 adult years shy

< Bonus Track >

Falling Like Leaves

can't verbalize my frustration;
can't visualize the expectation
of life— as a black man

in a game combating survival
as long as I can—
in seasons where our winters
come too soon

giving little time to prepare
to weather the weather—

so we hold still, & watch
green leaves transform into
caution's yellow stop lights, 'til
we toss & turn brown
under helicopter lights

&
        fall
    off
        like
leaves
            from
    trees

& mothers watch us sway in waves
'til we land on nature's graves

& dissolve into soil that
continues to fail & un-frail trunks
filled with modest treasure

incubating seeds for soon-to-turn
brown leaves to be the regularities—

for new generations' trees

making their expectancy rules
near levels of bees

after they lose tempers &
liberate their stings
& die too soon.

< 45 >

SINGLE MAMA BALLAD

< by m.a.t. } instruments- Proverbs 15:20 >

house title becomes prison
bond for teenage son seeking

magic wand. curfews are restricted
to few-s and former rules serve

as point of views. Then doctors
diagnose that single mama's mind will

nut up—but for teenage son— prison
arms open up.

peer pressured rebellions
suit his natural actions. dragging

mama's emotions down dirt road 'til
stress pays its physical tolls—

Then pastors preach that single
mama will soon backslide—but for teenage

son— devil's arms open wide.

weeknights carry weekend trends &
drugs secure role as dividends

tombs stone out thoughts of
shame. black face veils hide tears

of blame. Then psychics forecast
that single mama's soul is too weak—

after teenage son's grave
covered in dusk last week.

< 46 >

BUMPER STICKERS (A Nonet)

< by m.a.t. } instruments- Ecclesiasticus 30:1 >

never could an acne-full face nor
imperfect figure appease their laughs
especially in the comedy

club the school called third period class.
couldn't place any shining stickers

on inner value with self-worth in
the hands of everyone else— which is

where it lives 'til the growth change is felt.
only to become mad at the world—
including image of self, & those

fickle trans-parents— who never failed
to ask, "when will my student be the

child of the month?"   you probably would
not know what it feels like either to

try to build a life & future with
improper tools— tears get tired of
taking up for insecurity's

release. curiosity of this
thing called experimenting— block the

mind from spiritual peace. Only for
bullies & critics to give more than

their share. mad at everything that
seems unfair— including the change &
hormonal imbalance paving the

way— only for parents to not fail
to say, "don't forget to make straight-As!"

< 47 >
SIGN RIGHT HERE

< by m.a.t. } instruments- Nahum 3:1 >

the security guard asked if we
had been moving / though there was no
sign of a moving van /

when in fact / we were robbed—

never did anything to hurt or insult Trust
or her senses of safety / but we opened the
unlocked door / to see she packed her

belongings & moved / leaving walking trails on the
carpet / & hangers dangling in empty closets / wonder if
she spoke to them on her way out / or left before they

open the blinds to shine light on the little we
had / i'm sure they stepped over a few morals & family
values / moved aside thoughts of security / just to get

to the jewelry, video games & 4-year old
computer / they felt we no longer needed / they did
leave an invoice for us to sign off on the violation

felt / & mail it to the center-of-stereotypes that
manage apartment living / never again would I have
my own bedroom / knowing I was sharing my closet &

my toys / with faces I'd never be able to name / in some
form of a lineup / the police did find the dust from the guns
they carried / which floated like the feeling of invasion /

though no one saw what occurred / not even
Trust / only for the security guard to ask if we had
been moving / although there was no

sign of a moving van—
bless his heart / 'cause he knew
that brother knew /

& that hurt just as much.

<Interlude- On The Wall >

thugs ah-street
    talkin'

old men ah-fir coat
    mackin'

urban girls lips
    ah-smackin'

on route to their spots in' the hood.

white-t & jeans
    a-saggin'

education
    a-laggin'

urban pimps
    a-braggin'

baby strollers
    a-draggin'

back to the hood.

gold teeth
    a-shinin'

business just
    a-mindin'

girl behind
    a-watchin'

while clockin' their time in'
    postin'

on the wall.

FUNNY THAT WAY

< by m.a.t. } instruments- Galatians 4:3 >

1
eventually poverty becomes the mediocrity
        and scarcity's no random unfamiliarity;
and gang-bangers and thugs
        become as common as door rugs;
        2
and on the streets prostitution
        is a known institution;
while discriminations thrive like additions;
        3
and new mouths to feed
        roll out in numbers, like packs of weed—
        marijuana smoke blurring signs of hope;
        4
with the cost more than
the rate of return per day;
        unfortunately, life is funny that way.
        5
and the cries of the wife
        become the commodities of sacrifice;
and single parent homes
        become as common as the cell phones—
        the latest trend paying no dividends;
        6
with the overall effects spaced out
like the feigns' thoughts during the day;
        unfortunately, life is funny that way.
        7
with cardboard signs of needy
        as common as wall graffiti; though rims
and bass boom like shame off a mother's face;
        8
when her estranged son's sightings
        are a frequent as mosquitoes after West Nile bitings;
and broken bottles of rum
        provide fuel to boast about our slum;
        9
and tears fall barely more
        than police dogs knocking down the door—
        of a drug bust, of a cultural rust;
with the results immeasurable and
        translated through words even intellects can't say
        unfortunately, life is funny that way.

< 49 >
WISDOM EGO
< by m.a.t. } instruments– Deuteronomy 4:9 >

my parents have the
wisdom ego / rightfully
so / especially
with things they know / but fail to
realize I have also learned too /

sacrificed both in
myriad ways / so their son's days
would be filled with the
serenity they have helped
me attain / i love them so /

my mom and dad / and
people never forget to
remind them of my
possession of this old soul
they conclude I own (haven't

grasped the tangible
translation) but figured it
must be something of
conversational substance /
to all the people they have

spoken with since my
birth / and never forgot to
reply with the grand
role in their lives the son they
gave life to plays / little did

they know / I have washed
a face of wrinkles at age
fourteen / tested out
my first cane at eighteen / and
even plucked gray hairs off these

meaningless dreams in
recent days / despite moves and
words spoken that may
transcend my periodic
mortal age / i am still young /

still swinging on the
instabilities / still slide
down mental rebirths /
still like seesawing on my
foundation's basis / I am

adventurous / still
play checkers with weaknesses /
trade sporting cards with
vengeances / shoot billiards' pool
with mischievous / I am

ever-changing / still
play hide-n-go-seek with past
mentalities / and
scissors always dampen the
future's paper / the future's

paper will covers
my Rock of Ages / until
God moves / and transcends
my steps / and puts me back in
the perspective of whose son

I am / and where I
am in their collaborative
and divine life for
me / only reminding me
I am young / old soul or not

< 50 >

STREETS OF MANHATTAN

< by m.a.t. } instrument– Ecclesiasticus 9:7 >

You have me
for you, greatly

intrigued— amazed,
awakened as wonderland

is to Alice. Though
no blonde ambition,

no colorful
characters— just many

streets & avenues— to
the open-ended,

unconventional and
underexposed. For

timidity is no option
and weakness I am. I

saw you there. My
sheltered, overprotected,

and shielded vanity
mirror. In a dream-like

world staged on the
original insomniac

island. Our eyes
greet in disbelief

meeting and greeting
where the concept of

right and wrong no
longer exists. As the line

dividing fantasy and non
fiction evaporates. You

move uneasily as if
discomfort fits your

high rising size. Until
our hands shake

in verses of revelations—
devoid of hesitancy.

And I hear your voice.

< 51 >
GARBAGE OUTSIDE

< by m.a.t. } instruments- Colossians 3:19 >

  my married neighbors
leave their garbage outside their
  apartment door and

  the strings loosen— the
bags tear and the garbage spills—
  leaking remains of

  domestic violence
and pouring out all the words
  of vain and bruises

  of pain—for all the
tenants to see. with no shame
  shown, but silently

  until they remove
the garbage bags and dispose
  them—but each time they

  re-open the door—
we smell the same garbage spilled
  on the kitchen floor.

< 52 >

I TOO (AFRAID I AM)

< by m.a.t. } instruments- Ephesians 5:28 >

afraid I am,
when you hold me,
   afraid I am,
when you scold me;

afraid I am,
when you love me,
   afraid I am,
as you shove me;

/ I too once thought
  I was worth something

afraid I am,
when you have me,
   afraid I am,
when you grab me;

afraid I am,
when you greet me,
   afraid I am,
as you beat me;

/ I too once thought
  wedding bands meant something

afraid I am,
when you address me,
   afraid I am,
when you undress me;

afraid I am,
when you curse me,
   afraid I am,
as you hearse me;

/ I too once thought
  I would'vo done something

< Interlude: Channel Surfing >

in the swirl of millions
walkin' back & forth—
why am I here
alone?
large upscale apartment—
spectacular view
beyond the breathtaking cliché
twisted elegance— bitter beauty;
jazz echoing from
the surrounds of my speakers
through my blood vessels
down the untapped desires
mirroring emptiness—
why am I here
alone?
nothing like taking Metros to work
to return home to nothing
but emptiness—
& the remote control—
seeking the stimulant of conversation
& laughter— or hands in pants
pockets walking through
Central Park to return to
mirrored emptiness from a man
without a woman to hold
tossing, turning
as my hopes for love fade in the echo
of blowing taxi horns, alarming
sirens, and decade-old syndicated
TV shows— In need of someone to hold—
someone to grow then mold
into an eternal fixation
within my life

< 53 >
CYBER HICKEY

< by m.a.t. } instruments- Proverbs 14:13 >

confiding in you / replies of same,
so into you / don't even know your name;

/ running, rushing back /

to confess to you / open my convictions
   hidden identity / freed inhibitions;

giving in to you / no measurable pace,
   logging off your kiss / cyber hickey trace;

/ longing, craving for /

your words / descriptions on bare,
   messages instant / society unaware;

lonely seconds between / desires in secrecy,
   point of preparation / to breath into reality;

/ hoping, wishing where /

lurks the fear / for an identity untrue,
   no verification / image mirrors off you;

gasping sensations / of each thought read,
   caught in emotion / imagination's thread;

/ falling, stumbling back /

on words expressed / replies of same,
laughing out loud / don't even know your name.

< 54 >

SANCTUARY OF SIN

< by m.a.t. } instruments– Job 15:15 >

Tithes paid upon ye entrance—
 before midnight, ladies find
their fare free;
 en route to ride winds of the mood,
wild nights should be our luxury!

Tasting spirits before the alter call—
 all flavors of communion
in thee walls;
 saints shareth infamies less conviction,
& cuddle in pairs along sidewall halls

Offering to buy her communion—
 we break bread, giving
the alter our stay;
 fantasizing the postlude through dance movements,
as spirits of elation direct the way

Ah! the beauty of iniquity / in its sanctuary

Game calls for the biblical showcase—
 the phone books all the
disciples sport;
 capturing the verses & scrolls she lives by,
can't leave the temple, scripture short

Then celebration intersects ill-tempered saints—
 forcing the guards to halt
festivity;
 en route to fulfill the messenger's charge,
wild nights should be our luxury!

Spirit of heat couples thine lovers—
 topping off evenings
the undeclared goal;
 connecting under no string attached policies,
before thou spirit purges itself from thy souls.

Ah! the beauty of iniquity

< 55 >

INCREDIBLE HULK
< by m.a.t. } instruments– Ephesians 5:18 >

a coalitional tequila & vodka
make the evilest nemesis / it was

a martini & daiquiri special Friday
but my need sought a hero

with the clout to take me there /
instead I found myself babbling

& stumbling in irrelevance / held
captive in arms of an Escalade backseat /

'til I could kiss toilet seats / challenge
the call of cold showerings / &

spill all over the room / cool I am
happier hours later with the clutches of

experimentation in full gear / putting
long island ice teas / rum &

coke / & hunch punchers / out
of season / opening introductory

statements of your superpowers /
convincingly shared from the

tender of the bar /

forty bucks & thirty minutes in / I
hold your forth round in my hand /

becoming the universal expert / the
most generous tab on the ladies'

radar / & the cleverest shit talker / I
laugh at myself / it's cool though—

cause I'm there / eased nerves / &
freedom to converse, snicker, & kiss at

you without shame /

LIBRA SUNLIGHT

< by m.a.t. } instrument- Ecclesiasticus 9:8 >

the universe is filled with stars—but you
   strangely align to my soul in ways that
even the comfort of nature and
   conversations of zodiac constellations
that introduced you— seem to no longer suffice.

for my existence unconsciously sorted
   through your intricacies and convolutions
to create an uncomfortable place for me to
   rest my head—and listen.

 in the most astrological sense—for you,
   i am a mere malefic planet rotating
on a 25 degree axis with my rings

barely reaching toward any elements of voyage.
   you find me as a collection plate of innocence
and challenge—awaiting the right tithe to secure
   my soul in the nirvana of your choice.

(I greet you with correctness)

because even in my most benefic planetary
   moment—proclamations of naïveté and
introversion are unfound.

you are clearly tonight's stimulus— seizing
   my undivided, unrestricted attention— in
the worst kind of terrestrial way,

which leaves my mind constellating
   your conversations & my curiosity of
the nature of your comfort hoping
   you align my soul—
in the strangest-become-familiar ways.

< Interlude: Late Night Call >

gentle is thunder—
body awake; as my mind
sleeps— the phone excites
"come now," moistened clouds moan— and
lay down open skies for rain

< 57 >
ST. AUGUSTINE
< by m.a.t. } instruments– Proverbs 5:18 >

(adagio)

in the search for the fountain of
youth— to drink from its riches

to revive & rejuvenate every inch
of my liveliness— i've traveled the

distance, only to find my aim close
to home at the gem of the barer of

the Creator's creations. before our wine
glasses toast— my tongue encircles the lips

making chills up her spine stick to my
emotions like ice-cycles on walls— with no

sign of falling from my desires. I then
pour down the edges like water over

falls— causing more pressure as I near
the cascade— but first concentrate on

circling the circumference— like planets
revolve around stars (where the heat is

too hot to get any closer).

(allegro)

until I fixate her frame— like two Floridian
hills & begin to drink from the river flowing

between & rinse my head in the stream—

as I rock the boat hooked with an
anchor to ecstasy— holding onto her rails

until the fountain breaks through all dams,
all fronts and dampens the river

& the rain comes down.

GREATER THAN SENSES

< by m.a.t. } instruments- acapella >

let's fuse senses—

rub your hands on my shoulder—
    I need to feel your
 connection—

feel my grains of skin—thin as wafers
bleeding from the vital need of affection;

put your tongue inside my souls—
    I need to taste your
religions—

kiss away chardonnay flavored coal fires
fueled by any hesitation impressions;

(I will take you there gladly)

embrace the fresh fragrances of emotion
    I need to scent your
attention—

heed the burning lust within us
arousing all tensions through intervention;

be attentive for moans of instability
    I need to hear your
stimulation—

listen for needs of on-edge muscles
to sooth with strokes of relaxation;

view spirits refining my desires
    I need to see your
consecration—

rays of love outshining this moment
& resolving at the crest of culmination;

(silent as a breath)

< 59 >

POST-INAUGURATION (THE REMIX)

< by m.a.t. } instrument– Proverbs 31:10 >

(one, two, three, bass)

there's a poem in my head for you

a past-midnight while you dose off
& wonder why my movements
persist kind of poem

in this silent moment & the echo of
street cars   cargo trains
& airplanes hovering non-existent

with silence the addendum for the
aftermath of the inauguration

leaving room for the words of the
poem in my head for you
to formulate & craft notes for
instruments of your heart to understand

the things you'll need to know
to grasp & co-sign the moment you awake
read, then re-read, & call my office
to offer a response for what you
think my words say

it's better you know this now, but I tend
to distance myself from writing poetry
about writing poetry

but thought that if I could capture the
emotional battle I've dealt with &
inscribe the power & enormity of
love & passion within my sometimes
defensive & not-so expressive heart

& let my words serve as the instruments
to play the musical notes for you to
finally understand
then my writing just might be worth something.

see you tend to think the lives I've lived
have meant something— not realizing

that only now with you do I see why I've done
all I've done & worked for all I've worked for
you aren't feeling me— are you?

(drop the beat)

maybe I am a little ahead of myself—
but as a believer of chivalry
        I've learned the "whats" i must provide for...
the "hows" I am to go about...
        even the "wheres" in my life I must
be to find what you've already proven you'll give

only question I've had for those
who've stamped "eligible" across my pursuit
was for who?

& then you appeared...
without complexity, without sagacity,
without gates, without presentiment,

to claim not only my heart,
but my soul— before I even had
the chance to search for your ring

(bring the beat back)

i need you to know this & not
leave room for doubt   i need you
to follow me so I can love you the
way my heart desires

time after time   i've written each
line of the poem in my heart for you
until my own mind could understand
my feelings before I tried to use
my own poetic words as an instrument to
add to the beautiful music our lives make together

& after I engrave my past-12:45 a.m. while
you're sleeping in my bed (covered in my cologne
& shower gelled sheets) & wonder why I'm
not there holding you kind of poem—

my heart can then rest with yours too

< 60 >

COULD ONLY IMAGINE

< by m.a.t. } instruments– Ecclesiasticus 23:24 >

If she's not an angel, then I
    could only imagine
    what an angel might be;
For she's all the greatness the Word
    reveals of His celestial dynasty;

If her smile isn't sunshine, then I
    could only imagine
    how real sunlight would glow;
For her radiant smile sets the standard of beauty
    & no greater gleam any light could show.

If her kiss isn't heaven, then heaven
    must be some dynamic place;
For her love transfers straight to my heart,
    when her lips gently caress my face.

If her soul isn't wonderful, then I
    could only imagine
    if wonders could even be real;
Its that charm that drives me to her affection
    which is the model of infinite appeal.

but one thing she won't supply
    (although I'm sure her heart doesn't deny)
but reservations prevent her to say—

words to let imagination have its way;
    so I sustain & imagine—
if I could only love her; adore her;
    if I could only claim her; last-name her;

'cause If she's not my future, then I
    could only imagine
    what my future would hold;
for she's all the totality my life
needs to complete my partial soul;

my heart sighs—
my goose-bumps emerge;
my blood warms;
if you could imagine— if only you could.

< 61 >

NO GUARANTEE

< by m.a.t. } instruments- Proverbs 6:25 >

to want when you're not here
   to miss when you're so near
 my dreams that you fulfill—
    but your heart won't let you feel
the pain I feel   when I can't hold you now—

to leave with such urgency
   to give me no remedy
 to know   you may have someone else—
   deep inside are secrets kept
to spot other arms   that are holding you—

to pulse when I hear your voice
   to wait as you make your choice
 my fears that you won't come through—
    when no matter what I do
no guarantee   you'd come back for me—

to give with nothing in return
  to avoid a new wound to earn
 God my head is all screwed up—
    but yet, I won't give up
forcing a love   that might not be returned—

to freeze to num my pain
  to melt my hopes for gain
 my love has lost its core—
    as I stare at my heart's door
hoping you'd knock   to be let back in.

< 62 >

SIGN LANGUAGE (AFTER THOUGHTS)

< by m.a.t. } instruments- 2 Timothy 3:6 >

I just don't know—
one minute I want to leave,
the next minute I want to stay.

for I can't read where your heart is—
and I'm misinterpreting your
silent and subliminal messages
as a door existing between you and I

a door that's closed, and I'm
   without a key
   yet,

we've made friendships,
   we've hoped desires,
      we've shared intimacies,
         we've made ecstasies,
            and we've watch the passions
            of our bodies rise like the sun that rose
         as we laid in each other's arms
      then
after thoughts

became realities, and dreams
became recollections of what we shared—

we watched the alarm clock
tick away the time
for me to hold you tight.

though in bed, my body couldn't be still—
tossing and turning like the princess on the pea
on the uncomfortable feeling that

I confused your lust,
   with your heart
      and made you apart of my world,
         without any gravitational leverage
            to pull your feelings towards my affection.
         and my thoughts now ramble and shuffle,
      like your hands on my head when
   i geared in on your spot
while your legs first locked

my head—then my heart into place;
   without a key
   yet,

after I rise and we're face to face
   I confront feelings of inconsistency,
     feelings of confusion,
       after thoughts
         of acceptance were once here?
       that's why

I just don't know—
one minute I want you to stay,
the next minute I want you to go.

< Interlude: Ice Skating >

it was beautifully
crafted— their private passion slick like

ice and hidden like lines
of continuity that exist

between the skater and
the ice.   but she's slipping and I'm

capturing her secrets
and learning her moves— while I await

when the time is right to
blow their affair straight off the ice.

< 63 >

UNTIL TODAY

< by m.a.t. } instruments- Ecclesiasticus 25:17 >

…You'd think my heart sees something
my mind knows isn't there…

like your priority
like your attention & affection

though my eyes have always been
accused of being too hopeful— as I looked at

un-piercing walls & still tried to nail through them;
untamed forests & struggled to domesticate them;

& I'll admit— I can be overly optimistic at times.

which is why I tried to love you & only asked
that you love me too

like you said that you did— & so I believed.

now my mind is left to give my
heart something that's no longer there…

like openness
like warmth & even interest

& though my spirit has always been
accused of being too gated— as I looked at

broken hearts & tried to shield & guard mine;
preoccupied dreams of love & preventing them in mine;

& I'll admit— I've been overly protective at times.

which is why I tried to open up to love you & asked only
that you love me too…

like you said that you wanted to—
& swayed me to believe
& so I believed;

until today.

WHEN I JUST KNEW (A Rococo)

< by m.a.t. } instruments- Matthew 24:10)

When we see each other—
only silence & looks of perplexity
are exchanged;

When I just knew—
we'd still be dapping
each other up;

Only hoping we'd be at Falcons' games
In the suites with each other;
Or at Club Vision
gettin' it krunk with one another;

But instead—

We let a woman intrude the
years of friendship we formed;
then vile actions cut tides
& our reactions stormed;

Destroying that ideology
of friendship; Which is
something we all need;

Until you mixed friendship with women,
& add gossip & greed—
the results only foster negativity indeed;

When I honestly just knew
we'd still be boys;

Until our head nods
became rolling eyes—
& counterfeit smiles
formed the unanticipated disguise;

When I just knew—
we'd be at Mosley Park with
children named after each other;

Instead of hating on each other
& strategically avoiding one another

WE CARRY CAINS TOO

< by m.a.t. } instruments- Proverbs 17:17)

a weight of guilt and a hunchback to carry it on,
days of triumphs and nights of headaches latched on;
like six rainy mornings to my sunlit Saturday run;
when I've aimed to be something for everyone;
    (but, I've collapsed on stage)

forced to reassess people—
    without looking for smiles to see through,
'cause i've been told— We Carry Cains Too

a point of blame with a shadow-free doubt,
a destination unclaimed and this constant need for clout;
overextended workdays to reach ascendancy,
when I've suffer to give way for other's necessity;
    (but, I've disengaged)

forced to reassess purposes—
    without looking at souls to see through,
'cause I've been shown— We Carry Cains Too

inner circle of chairs but the stone wall where I post,
a salty great lake and a rocky mountain coast;
multiple mind marathons per each distress,
when I swarm in lost crowds and solitude less;
    (but, I've changed my mind)

forced to reassess places—
    without looking at maps to see through,
cause i've come to know— We Carry Cains Too

    (my blood cries from the ground)

< Interlude: Life Is >

life is easily irritable
    and forgets sometimes
we need to be free—

freedom is discriminatory
    and forgets sometimes
he needs not be so judgmental—

judgment is decisive
  and forgets sometimes
we're flawed and make mistakes—

mistakes are unforgiving
  and forget sometimes
we must continue to fulfill this life…

only to reflect on our decisions—
and what we've made them for…

only to look now at where life is
and why we're wanting more

< 66 >

FACES OF SHADOWS

< by m.a.t. } instruments- James 1:14 >

For you too— shall be
  shadowed; I barely know their
names; These Faces of
  Shadows— full moon lighting in
  to windows; lighting faces

of women without
  reasons here to be. How they
shape a light of our
  wedding rings— child-filled wombs from
  planted seeds; dreams of a soul

mate they think they see
  in me; though their thoughts are just
dreams and their Faces
  of Shadows only fill my
  sensual needs— as any

red-blooded human
  man; shuffling hormonal
needs and desires
  with spiritual fires, but
  unable to drop guards on

my insensitive
  ways— maybe that is why cold

bed halves; candles and
  incense in silent baths and
  emptiness now devour

my days— which lays me
  down in arms of you; (for you
too) shall be shadowed—
  I have hurt for love; danced for
  fools where pleasures lived— longing

for more than loves were
  willing to give— (looking to
favorite mistakes;
  bittersweet ruins; thorns of
  roses)— how I loved you; how

you easily hooked
  my sincerity to your
hearts; and cut the cords
  before our love could be born—
  aborting all my hopes and

dreams— with the morning
  after pills you fed me through
your conversations
  of regrets— right after you
  shadowed my face; so you would

not see the pain I
  would endure from the hurt you
would cause me to feel—
  for like warm-blooded women
  (who juggle sensual needs

and spiritual deeds)
  caught-up in your alluring,
yet devious ways.
  Confused on where to run and
  then writing me off as

evenings of fun— which
  brings my arms to you, For you
too will juggle in
  fires unwilling to tame
  with shadows of women names.

< 67 >

INK BLOT TESTING

< by m.a.t. } instruments– Leviticus 15:20 >

Cold Day.

Awaiting— A Clear Picture.

Hesitation, Anticipation,
Thoughts of Damnation And Reprobation
Dilute any Relaxation;

which it should.

because if Promiscuity
wasn't fused into Society
as a Normality

this Problem wouldn't be a Problem.

but it is— and we all partake from the forbidden fruit

but this is my Judgment Day, for me to await
and answer the question of modern-day Leprosies

as I sit,
Vacant, Crying spiritual Tears,
hoping society's Fears,

won't deem me one of the plagues wrenching
my generation's gears— and give me a positive response

giving way to spend each remaining day
in the midst of a gradual decay
so my head's all Confused and

Damnation and Reprobation
Diluting any Relaxation

which it should.

because if Promiscuity
wasn't fused into Society
as a Normality

this Problem wouldn't be a Problem.

< 68 >

EYES OF EVE

< by m.a.t. } instruments- Proverbs 4:18 >

If I can change contradicting forces
that reemerge at December's final hours—
I'd be able to halt my choices
from procreating & proliferating
with the adverse;

For change must necessitate somewhere—
& what more fitting an agent
then now. A lifetime of placidity
now crests souls at judgments when
the old lives no longer find welcome
mats— or at least want to resolute
a plan to;

As if the mysteries of
human overindulgences & iniquities
unraveled epiphanies at the Eyes of Eve
when the Gregorian Calendar resets—

which brings me here with optimism towards
bundling up leagues of light years &
conquering them all
once the full moons shift—

extra inches I carry— won't
cellulite my waist anymore;
unused gym membership— won't
avoid the workout crowds—
Sunday morning sleep ins— won't
avoid church services again;

leaving intermezzo style-desserts,
swings of personalities, rejection of
ecclesiastical tithing, & all that's adverse
outside the suitcases of things I must
bring pass the Eyes of Eve—
at least resolute a plan to—

only for her eyes to close & head
shake as I struggle to zip
excess baggage I'll still carry through.

< 69 >

PSYCHEDELIA PLEDGE

< by m.a.t. } instruments- Galatians 5:20 >

We like
    our ethanol & mescaline—
    with morning decaffeinate coffee beans;
    It brings us together—
    makes us conscious & prevents...

    ...our faces from shinning at the sunrise;
    ...street pigeons from feeding us crumbs of bread;
    ...our blood from giving us to the red colored crosses;

    & without— the dependency on
    the independency of the cliché
    for happiness

        (which is not worth the risk)

We like
    our ephedrine & nicotine—
    as the after work snack;
    It brings us relaxation—
    makes us calm & hallucinated, so...

    ...meadows of papaver somniferum won't sprinkle;
    ...mentalities won't anti-depress the bupropions;
    ...smog-filled air won't breathe our lungs into toxin;

    & without—dependency on
    the independency in the cliché
    of pleasure

        (which we can't risk)

    Balanced; Natural; Pervasive Meals—
    Nutritional, Herbal, & Euphoric;

We the Psychedelics—

    Dish not syndromes of life—
    Grill not tension nor Fry reality

    Broil not struggle nor Bake Depravities
    All which toxin our blood, organs,& nerve beginnings
    to prop endings of that feeling of stability—

We found
    a better way—
    Which brings us together—
    makes us allegiant & veneered
    & God-like;

    indivisibility—with liberty & euphoria for all;

    & without—dependency on
    the independency in the cliché of joy

        (which we prefer not toy)

    ...so our briefcases can carry us home from work;
    ...and our televisions can turn us on

& all is well

< Interlude: Asylum >

there's the usual—
      fields of stone walls;
pastures of wired fences;
      green sunny skies,
blue fields of sand,
      leather straightjackets
bar-thick window screens

making room for the unusual—
      warm-bloodedness;
ordinariness;
      abundance of sunlight,
reciprocals of trust;
      consistency of joy
offerings of peace

but
greeted by the usual—
hesitant hands

< 70 >
SUPPORT GROUP

< by m.a.t. } instruments- 2 Corinthians 6:9 >

So— what
brings
    You
       here?

trapped under vessels
    we don't tap   alone,
labeled   pathways
    to claim as our own—

though   we had no
    reasons here to be,
but when your appetite
    nods for leaves
from the   forbidden tree—

    there's no easy exit strategy.

And—
    You?

No shackles,
    Bars,
Nor locks—
    see buzzed or not—

    i couldn't leap high
enough to pull
    myself out
of the syringe my little life
    was placed in

though, it may have looked like a
    wishing well from a distance—
with images of dreams I continued
    to fulfill of   wide open sins
my injections fill

    look a-little closer;
just a-little bit closer;

you won't see   a ladder

    used to climb myself
in this cavity

and true   I had no
    justification there to be,
but when your appetite
     is forced to bob for crops
from the   forbidden tree—

    there's no easy exit strategy.

What
    About
You?

no obsession, but addictive,
    no placebo, but prescriptive
to the point that life
    becomes innate and routine

and spiritual gardens
    started nourishing seeds
dropped on my buds
    from the forbidden trees

and nurturing those
    seeds becomes the
false remedy

to save   a reliance that
    had no reason here to be—
but when your appetite
    grows a dependency of the
leaves off the   forbidden tree—

    there's no easy exit strategy.

Now— How
did
  I
    get here?

< 71 >

KISS FOR A RIVER

< by m.a.t. } instrument- Revelation 9:6 >

Knives that rest on shivering wrists, in fears,
Mirror image shaken by sorrowful eyes, in tears,
Cold bullets dance with hot temples, near ears,

...waiting on someone to rescue and reclaim.

Prozac and alcohol craving to intertwine,
Forward actions give no sudden time to rewind,
Building edges hold on when hope lets go to find,

...someone waiting to catch and redeem.

Guns lock between jaws to send salvation flying,
Misery become source for death's advocates lying,
Raptures sing notes near graves without crying,

...waiting on someone to care & esteem.

When caskets seduce comfort like hospices do,
And families and friends won't see through,
A damaged soul with a pregnancy test turned blue,

...waiting on someone to come deliver me...

From the incompleteness that my life feels,
The spiritual separation my faith reveals,
The capacity that can't afford depression's bills,

...waiting on someone
    to stop me from kissing this river of pills.

< 72 >

SEPARATE BEDS

< by m.a.t. } instruments- Titus 1:15 >

we're a multiplicity—trying to get our
collection of selves on one accord.

once a believer in living forever—
once wanting to know everything;

but if our way goes our way— tonight

we'll awake to blood on our hands
knife wounds at our past

gunshots towards the futures i've once
wanted to slay and never let them see.

back when I believed I'd live forever
& thought I could learn everything

'til separate beds split the mold—

& one of us started Storming the Heavens
and mystified the others.

once a believer in utopianism—
once wanted to love everyone,

but if our choice is our choice— tonight

we'll awake to nature-run wild across turbulent
skies— that never looked so blue, even in darkness

back when I wanted to be something for everyone
& thought all people could love me

'til we knelt to separate beds—

allowing one of us study the Encyclopedia of Un-Belief
and confused the others.

trying to get our selves collected
on one accord— the

multiplicity that is.

< 73 >

SICK (RED EYES)

< by m.a.t. } instruments- Mark 4:19 >

I've become so worried;
so suppressed;
so lost— so stressed

I've become physically sick.

coughing, chocking on thoughts of preconception;
sneezing, wheezing on specks of reprobation;
awaiting The Living Word's healing for my soul;
disgrace & contentment hover, while destructions unfold;

itchy throat of words of damnation said;
achy ears of sounds of sinful actions alleged;
head throbs with thoughts of desperation;
nose running with ticking time past expiration;

gazing at the mirror—red blood fills my eyes;
miserable until The Spirit reveals devils in disguise;

Then...

The redness shows The Blood covering my life;
pacing away from sickness—felt eternally in-sight;

though my legs & knees feel so frail, so weak;
as His hands give me strength as they reorder my feet;
to make growing in His word—my purpose, my aim;
rejoicing in the victory—He tells me to claim;

eyelids flash images of Him hauling me over strife;
and The Crucifixion of the Lord—so I'd one day have life;

once so worried;
so lost— so stressed

no longer misguided and feeling suppressed.

< 74 >
LIFE FOR BEGINNERS
< by m.a.t. } instruments- 2 Timothy 2:22 >

There's so much unspoken
I've carried for years— that
speaks through

the path I love— the path I transform;

even the disconnected mercurial energies
existing between myself and
those I've let within

(though faith never showed me this)

There are tears unshed
I've held for years that
rain rivers through

the path I judge— the path I express;

even the barricades erected
between the experiences of my life
and those I create them with

(though no one ever said a thing)

There's a level of growth that halted until
now which plant seeds of disbelief
beneath your mysterious branches, about

the path I hermit— the path I perish;

even the jupiterian energies
of judgmental analyses towards the boy I was—

looking at the man
I've learned I can not grow to be

(though this enlightenment is all new to me)

All this said— so my child-like immanence
can relive youth; follow the pillar of mercy;
and outgrow;

Yet— I have this anxious feeling of watching
school-aged seeds play for the first time

discovering tarots— discovering love;

The right way. Mind at Recess;

Looking at them swing— looking at them
reach for mysticism; Then

swinging on spheres transcendently
I become apart of them too;

unsure if swinging with me is something
you'll want to do—

before I can head back to class.

< Interlude: A.M. Meditation >

Reverse commotion
before dawn—

let me breathe
comfort into your pain

& run worries over my
stretching relief until it breaks

& pours beauty & blissful peace

through my lungs, my blood, my muscles—

I take a deep breath—

as my mind breeds with tranquility

and cuts me from the umbilical cord of
reality that feeds us—

I exhale— and begin the day.

< 75 >
UTENZI OF FURAHA

< by m.a.t. } instruments– Isaiah 30:26 >

Morning sidamo coffee mugs
   adjust easily to sun jazz sets—
usually night insomnia would find
   Western-world pinned television
Infomercials yawning to the cricket
   croons on amplified microphones—

but no confinement or concept of time—
only rest
only furaha—

leaving the warmth of caffeinated
   sidamo mute & the Swahilian
retreat breathing room for the
   reconstruction of the scenic harmony
before the 5th day of Wahabu's creation—

and how good it is.
how good it is;

Morning showers adjust inertly to
   twilight mists that blanket the Maravi—
usually night fishermen rods sway
   to unopened bahari eyelids
which would only loosen from strokes
   of dusk's water keen

but no necessity or delineation of time—
only rest
only furaha—

leaving dawn moisture handshaking
   moonlight rays & the Swahilian
heritage assembly lines to recreate
   the gwaride route of nature
before Wahabu's 5th day—

and how good it is.
how good it is;

alone with Him.

< 76 >

♩108♩

FAVORITISM AMONG BIOMES

< by m.a.t. } instruments- Deuteronomy 8:15 >

Maybe I was adopted—
& haven't been

informed— But Mama Earth
shows favoritism.

She allows Grassland to herd
massive populace & graze animals—

To be tamed & domesticated.
Tundra inherited the eyes to unlock

the poles— Stemming resilience &
specialty too radiant to greet

just any common eye. Forest keeps
the intricacy & soil richness

we all borrow from— When
it's time to develop into ripeness—

to appease the most temperate
beauties— Seeking the provider

of the terrain of home (somewhere
I failed to mention Mama

had four boys). Which leave
me the youngest as the most latitudinal &

arid of them— Desert.

Oceans find me least attractive—
Preferring the richness of my

eldest brother & atmospheric winds
find my humor & jokes too dry

to entertain. While my brothers
inherited Mama's wit & exotic beauty— I'm

left tanning my skin in the heat
of the sun— With no rainfall planned

'til 2045 when we expect Mama's water
to break & birth another ocean—

(somewhere I failed to mention Daddy
left before I was born).

Never found out why— So I've
always thought I was some form of

an ecological mistake—
So I'm not sure if it's favoritism

or if I was adopted— & have yet to
be informed.

wonder if Global Warming
could've been my father

Too?

< 77 >
TREES IN SEATTLE
< by m.a.t. } instruments- Psalms 1:3 >

what kind of tree would I be? would I plant roots
in red southern clay / & spread like 19th century
thoughts of concession / when I disagree
with confederates who forever ruined

the banks of Mississippi's river / & watched
its prosperity pour down drains / allowing its
dollars to transfer to the French quarters
of Louisiana / Well— If southern heritage fits

my destiny / that's where my roots would be /
Then again— I could find home on a Boston street corner
/ springing through cement & asphalt walkways / making
all my replenishments / human-induced /

for I couldn't dare be in New York City / might be
estranged in the Greenwich Village / decorated

with cigarette buds in a Jersey hood / or go dry
with the art of the Harlem Renaissance /

well— if New England culture / holds my place
/ that's the ground soil my roots would
face / could fit near Lake Superior / fall
bitter in frost / dying off like Midwestern manufacturing

jobs / leaving us to call on commercialized holydays
/ to fill voids of Winter wealth memories /
But in Nebraska & Kansas / I'd have to stand
strong / because when i rub nature wrong /children

of flowers will hold their tongues / watching
tornadoes scoop me up like vacuums /
& dropping me without leaves & shame / opening
my skeletal fragility / for news cameras

to blast my once-covered natural defenses across
TV screens worldwide / well if the flat plains lay
down for my space / that's the soil my roots would
embrace / palm trees in Southern California glow with

the lights reflecting their surroundings /
& are easily photogenic / like the stars & lounge bars
that place them in spotlights / to shine with / but they
keep away all alphabetical names of hurricane winds

/ but get next to no attention / nested in an Alabamian
forest or Arizonian desert / But- the clout of trees
is that we can be wherever you want us to be /
& if the San Fernando valley fits my destiny / that's

where my roots would grow for me /
In Seattle / trees withstand the rain / & does
it pour / only for it to pause / & nature send a
request for more / so the trees flock together like

Nigerian villages after rites of passages / cause
they carry strength like legacies / & pass their powers
to generations through fables and tales / that
only trees that withstand rain

/ can celebrate in.

< 78 >

OFTENTIMES

< by m.a.t. } instruments– Jubilees 2:12 >

Oftentimes— I am
reminded I had more than
a friend in you— On Good Days...

I embrace comfort;
welcome recollection; and
again feel the Hawaiian

breezes of love felt
strolling along Waikiki
beach— my smile reveals hand in

hand—gentle is night;
i feel closer to the light.
(smile within you)— On Bad Days...

I see departures;
the return to nine-to-fives;
and disappointment reminds

me of how it will
forever shake your hand with
mine— in the handshakes only

two distant souls of
meadow filled Oahu country
land can understand— for the

darkness of moonlight
to reveal— (handshakes at sight);
i feel closer to the light.

< 79 >

AMERICA TO REDEFINE

< by m.a.t. } instruments- For Martin Luther King, Jr. >

Our legacy overcame a struggle,
   Heroic deeds resonate on wings of time;
MLK breathed life for his dream,
   And handed manhood America to redefine.

But his charge has rested in a time capsule,
   And like dreams, we've seen no revelations of the end;
An end to inequality and birth of harmony,
   So divided we stand, united we bend.

The capsule holding the dream has been buried,
   Buried within the hearts of which we sing;
Anthems for warfare and cries of uncertainty,
   Chorused by the weight of what troubles bring.

For our frustration is built by resistance,
   And our complacency floats on wings of time;
MLK marched on against opposition,
   And handed manhood America to redefine.

When broken wings leak complacency,
   And it rains into our thoughts conceived;
Halting sands in the hourglasses of change,
   Giving birth to rebels for the once believed.

Then contentment sprouts in lands of ignorance,
   And rebels wash their attack on silent shores;
Until reality of a united state now bending,
   Knocks its awareness on manhood's doors.

Outlining paths for us to step to the plate,
   And bask closure on all doubts in our mind;
Because, MLK gave his life for our dream,
   And in his will, left America to redefine.

< Bonus Track >

Re-Countin' On You

In this battle—
To keep Bushes

from growin' back in
the Evergreens of

universal growth—
Crafted by Clinton

who paved forests to build
walkways for all—

but Tropical storms
dampened skies— As his

popularity fell— Like his
pants— When one

intern stepped to
satisfy the Man—

When his wife— and
hand could no

longer suffice. We're
re-countin' on you

Florida— as two
tenders of the bar

battle it out— While
their bipartisan patrons sip

on false spirits
of divided uniformity—

Like broken handcuffs
in need of the same

key— To solve
our problems.

< 80 >

TRUST FALL

< by m.a.t. } instrument– Isaiah 9:3 >

people jump from twin towers without gear;
  as smoke grows with no hope to disappear;
firsthand account of the commence of our fear;
  from terrorists who die with no sympathy near—

shock spreads like cement falling down;
  smoke creates faces of evil who frown;
satin's triumph arisen from underground;
  as America's security comes tumbling down—

and begins
    falling,
       falling,
          fall—
      ready?

    "No," a nation says.

then Trust falls…

as our citizens die instantly in gloom;
  images of shock flood our living rooms;
with no idea of next intention for doom;
  retaliations of hate, our thoughts presume—

economy loses basis at the skip of time;
  eyes lock at footage to vanguard our mind;
skyscrapers shaking workers home— only remind;
  that America's actions have amassed the fine—

leaving fear of unthinkable to hover in midst;
  affluent stirred to loosen philanthropy's fist;
world hears repercussions of a terrorist's hiss,
  wondering how we let things come to this?

HANDSHAKES ACROSS THE GLOBE

< by m.a.t. } instruments– Revelations 5:13 >

Journey from the Wall of China to the Atlantic,
    Toss a link from Jerusalem to Italy;
Export Colombian coffee beans to Spain,
    Stretch your smile back
for Germany;

Bring Brazil on a hike to the Himalayas,
    Play hide-in-the-Pacific with Japan;
Carry Liberia to the Eiffel Tower,
    And bring back French wines
to the Motherland;

Pour the oils of Iran on Canadian steel,
    To loosen a course from Greenwich to a Caribbean beach;
Take the snow cones of the coldest Arctic,
    To cool the tensions of
the Middle East.

Negotiate with Russia, but teach them the song
    Of an African village and an Indian groove;
And as you walk the streets of Hong Kong,
    Recollect teaching Netherlands
a salsa move.

Small gestures to harmonize our world,
    Could be as easy as teaching Australia to electric slide;
And when you're hitch-hiking back to England,
    Nigeria will offer you
the ride.

< Interlude: Recipe For Soldiers >

dish: Soldiers for War

recipe: take the 30s' depression
/ mix with the 80s'

regression / sprinkle wars of
the 40s & teens / & stir

in the 50s' & 60s' inequalities /
sample tastes of earlier

times / like 90s' songs / &
shower in the 70s' social

& political wrongs / Now stir—

'til the distinction of times
dissolves / then sense

security to feel issues
were resolved / then cover

& heat with fear.

< 82 >

WAR PROCLAMATION

< by m.a.t. } instruments- Psalms 24:6 >

Mr. President?

Whereas, questioning your dilemma of pace
                seems a step out-of-place;
Whereas,   asking where motives derive
                become words bipartisan structures keep inside;
Whereas, probing your self-aspiration
                fuels media backlash across the nation;
Whereas,   inquiries of contrived fear
                seem like steps out of political gear;

"...is it just me, or is it hot in here?"

Whereas,   those cultured in fear won't believe
                any evidence that's been deceived;
Whereas,   bombs were prepared to fly
                before those commanded understood why;
Whereas,   egotistical gains hidden in plain sight
                are used to justify war to stem peace is right;

"...is it just me, or are these spotlight too bright?"

Whereas,   manufacturing a pressing need to deploy war
                are blinded by the tediousness I'll be fighting for;

Which is?

< 83 >
FLOATING IN THE DEAD SEA

< by m.a.t. } instruments– Jeremiah 12:7 >

i too shall one day feel old,
   when my ashes brush their feet in the sea;
chills of death pull flesh afloat,
   wishing you could float with me.

i too shall one day walk weak,
   when my bones connect to rub way;
chills of friction deepen reaction,
   wishing my life didn't accrue warfare's pay.

i too shall one day feel my soul,
   pouring its weight on the drear of my chest;
pulses beating at speeds of walking canes,
   wishing headstones would mark my quest.

i too shall rinse my spirits into the sea,
   and thrust all aches to the enemy's floor;
as three Comets fly across the sky,
   lighting the tunnel to the other Shore.

i too shall one day grow instantly gray,
   when my urn faints into the sea;
tragedy floating in blood of the Lamb,
   wishing you could float with me.

< 84 >

THE SOLDIER'S FUNERAL

< by m.a.t. } instrument–Jeremiah 9:21 >

tragedy mirrors sunlight;

silently walking away— offering awareness
tears pouring through moving emotions

hurt causes inquiry

questions ask why?

eyes covered
   hands in faces
heads shaking

sorrowfully filled eyes to call
on Comforter—

 the home going.

(the soldier's funeral)

going home, the Comforter on
call to eyes filled sorrowfully

shaking heads
faces in hands
covered eyes

why ask questions?

inquiry causes hurt

emotions moving through pouring tears
awareness offering— away walking silently

sunlight mirrors tragedy;

HEAVEN'S GLORY

< by m.a.t. } instrument- Luke 10:20 >

No glory found in tragedy,
    With eyes denying pain-filled tears;
As waterfalls halt over masses of hurt—
    Where a loved life fuses with our fears.

We must not question God's purpose,
    Though comfort won't comfort the empty space;
And during this period of bewilderment—
    Remember— they're in a better place.

For God is too wise and too trustworthy,
    To give leverage for any one mistake;
The King of Kings would never consent—
    A burden our families could not take.

So feel the angel wings of consolation,
    Wipe away any outpour of tears of sorrow;
And feel the radiation of a lost smile—
    That we'll hold in the distant tomorrow.

Even with the void that fills our hearts,
    Unable to wholly vanish or erase;
They now wear God's crown of paradise—
    Forever resting in a better place.

Heaven is rejoicing that our angel
    Is now without hurt and melancholy;
For they have been deemed eternal life—
    And our tragedy, is heaven's glory.

< 86 >

AT JUDGMENT DAY

< by m.a.t. } instruments- Proverbs 15:27 >

say goodbye—
walk away from insufficiency,
bearing no cross of weakness;
opposite pain—
imaging sights of paradise,
with no reflections of meekness;

(chorus) see, He knows we strive to be our best—
    but rate our own success on another man's scale.
    only to realize in th End, it didn't even matter,
    whether self-investments posted their bail.

sought comfort—
hiding in far off places
of distance spaces;
expensive tastes,
left empty spaces within
those foreigners' places;

(chorus) because we journeyed near and far—
    craving comfort, in quest of a global home.
    only to realize in the End, it didn't even matter,
    whether cultures clashed or offered atone.

so obsolete—
the insignificant things
that hurdled up our esteem;
allowing thoughts—
of desperation to appear
much closer than they seemed;

(chorus) because such precious moments were lost—
    seeking glory in places reluctant to give,
    only to realize in the End, it didn't even matter,
    if we embraced a red carpet-life to live.

(ad lib) at the Judgment Day—
    those irreverent metals of praise
    we've consumed;
    matter not—
    and remain outside
    doors of Deliberation Room.

< 87 >
THE REMISSION
< by m.a.t. } instruments- Malachi 2:9 >

Un-hide our past—
    & let the world see the pain caused for so many years;
Un-cover our ancestors' anguish—
    & take a walk down their trail of tears;

Un-hinder our power—
    & erase the need to fight for civil rights;
Un-darken our political strength—
    & honor our leaders who stood for what was right;

Un-conceal our heroes—
    & place them back into the history books;
Un-claim our historic figures—
    & give us back credit for the people you took

Then claimed as your own...

    Like Cleopatra & other heirs of the throne.
    Let the world see how great we are,
        was & will always be;

        & stop telling a story that's incomplete—
    for we won't stop fighting until we can feel,
    that the perception of our past is accurate & real.

    Point taken?   Lest we forget— Lest we forget!

Un-discourage our fathers
    Un-break apart our race;
Un-exclude our achievers

    Un-distort the look of our face;
Un-deny us the right to vote
    Un-create negative connotations for "black;"

Un-illiterate our inner cities
    Un-slash scars across our grandfathers backs;
Un-enslave millions of our natives

    Un-whip all the wounds that we caught;
Un-auction off our forefathers
    Un-educate your children superiority thoughts;

Un-ship us across from the motherland
     Un-kill off millions of our brothers;
Un-separate our people's youth

     Un-rape everyone of the king's mothers;
Un-twist the story about our past
     Un-instill the anger & resentment we know;

Un-due all the things we would've never done
     & maybe you'll see the pain go.

< 88 >

REPARATIONS

< by m.a.t. } instruments- Romans 20:29 >

well past
youthfulness— he
knew how to avoid the
staleness of life; tediousness
of time

gone by—
considering
he survived the global
war fares levied by the needless
mistakes

of the
western wing-pinned
presidential egos
and contradicting confusion
caused by

unclear
economic
equalities— though his
armed force service and modest life
never

sought the
reimbursement

for the mules his fathers
never received— did own and tend
forty

acres
of heritage—
knowing he would not be
the one to gracefully mow its
lawn or

shower
its meadow fields—
so he spent seventy
plus years to pre-plant the soil; and
pre-pick

weeds; while
fertilizing
and grand-fathering seeds
that would sprout and celebrate in
the fields

he would
never live to
reap— but sowed legacies
and memories our little lives
would keep.

< Interlude: Tomato Soup >

Miss Ruth represented everything
America refused to be—
most notably color blind.
In nineteen eighty-five, I
became a strong
believer
then, that
the
sixteen
point seven
million colors
of citizens in
the grand spectrum of light
hid the under-developed

land in their home country which is
how two brown-eyed Western Michigan

children discovered golf clubs, snails, the
golden girls, vintage clothes, hand-me
down coloring books & crayons,
tomato soup, and the
quintessential worth
of elderly
souls. outside
tv
screens
and a
country-town
American
kindergarten class—
fragmented culture &
color blind eye lenses never
seemed oblivious— unfit for
realities of America.

< 89 >

WOMEN, BE YE

< by m.a.t. } instruments- 1 Peter 3:7 >

Women,

Be ye feminine;
Be ye fruitful;
Be ye flirtatious;
Be ye fettered;

But
Be not fanatic;
Be not forceful;
Be not free;

But Women

Be ye heartfelt;
Be ye humanitarian;
Be ye hesitant;
Be ye helpful;

But

Be not honcho;
Be not hedonistic;
Be not historical;

But Women

Be ye musical;
Be ye magical;
Be ye minute;
Be ye moveable;

But
Be not masculine;
Be not maneuvering;
Be not militant;

Go ahead—
Sing ye hymns
until Aurora comes,

No home for your throne
in Man's kingdoms

for your militarism;
for your activism;
for your radicalism;

But Women,

Be ye obedient;
Be ye oppressed;
Be ye obscure;

But,
Be not overbearing;
Be not opposing;
Be not orderly;

Sing ye hymns
until Aurora arrives—

Cause no space
for your place

Through Man's
narrow eyes.

SIMILAR EXCITEMENT
< by m.a.t. } instruments- For Halle Berry >

I'm sure—
You were dressed in the Similar Excitement
Dorothy Dandridge wore / True your hair

and Elie Saab dress were set to be a credit to
the race / But the race hadn't won in 74 years

of competition / Yet tired of runnin' then comin' up
short each year / As Hollywood strobe lights

would cheer / Then we'd shed an early
twentieth-century cinematic-like tear of defeat /

In silence—
Walkin' the stars of fame with our heads
hung down / Wondering why we couldn't cut

the ribbon and make Hollywood Boulevard
gleam just a little black-light brighter /

Diana Ross and Cicely Tyson sounder tranquil
blues / Purple-turned black skies color-in works

of Diahann Carroll and Whoopi Goldberg /
Soundless pianos dance music

One decibel above Angela Bassett's
golden-screen voice / Pearls around your

neck / as you leaped into the Academy race in
the final stretch / holding the performance

to roll the red carpet over stars who dreamed for
the one thing time wouldn't let them see;

And your face—
Gave tears of modesty as you broke the
barriers of history /

Carrying our hearts along through /
Know we cried past midnight alongside you.

< 91 >

HEIRS OF ALPHA

< by m.a.t. } instruments– Hebrew 13:1 >

The light shaped by an unyielding seven—
& evinced through generations
      Who choose to believe;

We offer you access into the bond we cherish—
So open your life &
      Prepare to receive.

The greatness ended not at the inception—
But continued to spawn legacies to
      Transcend & uphold—

No other sands set aflame to initiate—
Would drape you in the
      Powers of the black & gold.

Though a heritage of pioneering & distinction—
Must not rest in the ritual
      Nor in its past—

For it's up to you to sustain the legacy—
& scion movements for
      Believers to surpass;

In my hand is the key to its vitality—
Packaged with service & love
      For humanity—

Although massive— the gift shall never lay heavy—
If allegiances are pledged
      Through humility;

Now close your eyes while carrying the flame—
Then pledge to the challenge to
      Forever ignite—

Then you'll too own the legacy of Alpha—
      & strengthen the core of
      our fraternal light.

< Interlude: Lesson Plan Oath >

(for our young sons)

Learn to count joy,
  Before storms pass;
Know to claim victory,
  When my talents seem last;

Aim to keep a smile,
  In the negative lights;
Secure daytime safety,
  In the dangerous nights;

Learn to play all positions,
  In a game with no teams;
When doubts try to lead,
Learn to follow my dreams;

Avoid failure in my classes,
  And promise to do my best;
Then save time for service,
  In my periods of rest;

Learn to build castles of success,
  Without grains of sand;
And as my childhood fades,
  I'll become a strong man.

< 92 >

GONE INSTEAD

< by m.a.t. } instrument– Psalms 73:26 >

1. Stumble into debasement?
Claim joy while secularly fed?
Tumble in unforgiveness?
— I'd be gone instead.

2. Measure up to nothing?
Find confrontation with fear?
Drown in ripples of self-regret?
Rest assure— I'd disappear.

Chorus: no room to misfire;
no time to waste time;
no comfort in comfort;
no time to serve time…

…giving birth to fallacies
and testing for knowledge
of the book of wisdom
which I haven't read /
see— I'd be gone instead.

3. Give into instabilities?
Hide revelation within my sleeve?
Be broken into misconceptions?
Guarantee— I'd first leave.

4. Costume my shield & cross?
Live by doctrines I can't convey?
Yield to evil's degeneracy?
I couldn't— I'd walk away.

Chorus: no regret to regret;
no time to waste time;
no endurance for endurance;
no time to serve time…

…opening ears for guilt
and shame outlined in
the book of wisdom
which I haven't read /

I'd be gone instead.

< 93 >

A FRIEND, WITHIN

< by m.a.t. } instruments- Ecclesiastes 4:10 >

bid adieu— to not knowing how to love,
you've shown me that,

bid adieu— to not learning when to cry,
you've taught me that;

using your heart to spark
   my growth within;
now I've found a friend, within
   this chaotic world we're
living in— and it's you.

bid adieu— to no need to hide behind my smile,
you've open my inner glow,

bid adieu— to the thoughts of feeling semi-empty
this life had come to know;

using the light of God
   you possess within;
now I've found a friend, within
   this hectic world we're
living in— and it's you.

If our friendship ever deems
   miles of distance in between,
if new careers enter our scenes,
   and craft opportunities to grow between;

you'd have a special place in my heart,
   and in my memories,
you'd hold an integral part
   to the joys I'd recall.

because I found a friend, within
   this crazy world we're living in—
and it's you.

< Bonus Track >

Ideology of Friendship

1
if my life was to unfold into a book—
you would know each chapter & be one of
the guardian angels characterized
who helped me discover the strength within to
conquer my fears.

2
if I was to crumble into puzzle
pieces you would know how to reconstruct
me through your friendship & ongoing commitment

3
If I was to live to tell any pain
burning within— I'd find condolences
in your trembling eyes from my spirit's
wounds— that you'd too scar from.

4
if my world was to come tumbling
down, you'd be there to catch my distresses
in your natural eminence.

5
If my soul mate appeared— I know you would
be standing by my side or in the crowd holding
my spiritual hand as we
walked into this new venture together.

6
for I am never alone— because you
are the ideology of friendship—

maximizing the limits of ascending
lines of infinite memories & good
times & days when I am reminded of
how your spirit shines & my spirit glows

7
because of you.
and with one glimpse of the smile you show— it
continues to let me know— the reason I love life so—

and that's friendship.

< 94 >

SOUL MATED

< by m.a.t. } instruments- Psalms 151:2 >

would've been sharing my heart—
   but I held my emotions
fearing you'd feel
   too connected;

would've been losing control—
   but I held my feelings
so your heart wouldn't
   feel subjected...

to be all I truly wanted us to be;
   so somewhere, somehow
I convinced myself
   you weren't the one for me.

would've been baring my soul—
   but I held my religion
hoping you wouldn't
   feel soul mated.

would've been offering my love—
   but I held my hand
knowing you'd then
   feel obligated...

to be all I dreamed we could be;
   so somewhere, somehow
I held my tongue
   on speaking our love's prophecy—

 until God spoke your name.

< 95 >

THAT RIB AROUND MY NECK

< by m.a.t. } instruments- Ephesians 5:31 >

God   I'm lonely.

make me a wife—
reckon her my companion
mate our souls as a union;

and order her steps toward my heart.

God   make her a catalyst

for my everlasting happiness
and let me breathe the air of love
as her spirit humidifies my empty life
like only a woman can...

God   create a wife for
this lonely man.

for I haven't found the love of my life quite yet
and on a string of failed attempts hangs
that rib around my neck.

God   let us create a love child—

i want to see our love's reflection in his eyes;
and watch him become a man before my eyes;

and order his steps toward Your word

God   make him an adhesive
for keeping our family unbroken
as his youth inserts a joy
into our lives that only a lovechild can...

God   mold a family
for this lonely man.

for I've found wealth and success
which are both linked on the string
holding that rib around my neck.

and it's getting heavy on this empty heart

< 96 >

COLUMNISTIC SOUNDS

< by m.a.t. } instruments- Titus 2:15 >

Sometimes I see Voices—

Shaken and Fragile
        voices;
Reclusive and Illusive
        voices;
Echoic and Intense
        voices;

offering counsel for my
        choices;

        without Tact (less intrinsic);
without Frame (less forensic);

so my eyes must drown the tones,
        of the columnistic sounds;
focus on directing my talent,
        where my heart is found.

Sometimes I hear Hands—

Directive and Instructive
        hands;
Mindful and Molding
        hands;
Suppressive and Subjective
        hands;

offering retunes for my
        plans;

        without noise (less liberty);
without innateness (less identity);

my life must take the lead,
    to stage and master my ambition;
focus on directing my future,
    from the sound of intuition.

< Interlude: I Envy >

1

I envy cumulus clouds—
Who glide earth thin of stress;
I envy morning sunrises,
Who rise high
        with no pass of tests;

2

I envy lily pads—
Who glide water like Saviors do;
I envy the leaping frogs,
Who hop lilies
        with no falling through;

3

I envy sugar canes—
Who please senses with no imprints;
I envy grains of sands;
Who craft steps
        for man's footprints;

4

I envy tree branches—
Who reach out on faith, with eyes closed;
I envy Mr. Atlas,
Who mapped plot
        to discover uncharted roads.

ANTENNA-FREE

< by m.a.t. } instruments- Proverbs 3:24 >

When it is finally mine—
      this hope, this rhetoric,
      this periodic element of earth
we supposedly acquire with age as
the tide for out-of-sync waves
even as the ignition for idle bridges—

so we can have, not just hold.

Where I am not heavy—
      but lightweight & liberated,
      unconventional & cultivated;
digital clearness
even through analog dependency

fully receptive, antenna-free.

When it is finally triumphant—
      this war, this revolution,
      these gladiator-style battles
we supposedly hoard resources,
right-of-passage our youth,
& allocate bodies-to-bag—

so we can live freely, not just exist.

Where I can lay me to rest—
      undisturbed, devoid of fear,
      detached yet crystal clear;
high frequency of signals
but perfect clarity

internally receptive, antenna-free

this man will feel at home.

< 98 >

ATLANTA IS MY HOME

< by m.a.t. } instruments- Exodus 21:13 >

face like sweet potato pies
   full of auburn avenue's history;
face like civil right movements
   civil wars with battles for equality;
face like stone mountain's engrave
   remembrance of southern cultures arrive;
 face like hot kitchen ovens
   too hot summers to play outside;

American is my legacy,
   Georgian is my family,
red dirt held a life sown,
   Atlanta is my home.

face like Harlem's thrills
   West End cooks up cultural flavors;
face like Beverly Hills
   Buckhead strips cruise expensive savors;
face like Centennial Olympics
   venues and parks remind of glorious days;
face like phoenix from ashes
   arisen from fires less marks of rays;

American is my ideology,
   Georgian is my civility,
hospitality in flesh and bone,
   Atlanta is my home.

face like congestion
   traffic stacking frustration on Grady curve;
face like Moses' following
   churches find figures in high reserve;
face like corruption
   political leaders secure their destinies;
face like high rising buildings
   success sliding in reach for our families;

American is my mannerism,
   Georgian is my bio-rhythm,
southern wombs carried me too long,
   Atlanta is my home.

ANCESTRAL SOUL FEAST

< by m.a.t. } instruments- Numbers 29:39 >

Heart toward reciprocity
seeking tools of ancestral souls
to stir up spirits of
Grandma's Sunday after-church dinners—
& make her remembrance proud.

Where the dire need for the unification
of generations weakens imperial energies,
obstructs the tilted rotation of
this sphere we know as Earth—

Giving me halted time to invite
the elements of soul & wonders
of food to bring us home—
& together.

Table set; Silverware down—
the screen door opens for...

New York-pinned Fried Chicken,
coming from M&G Diner;

New Orleans-kitchen sink Gumbo,
arriving from Harbor's;

Chicago-broiled Collared Greens,
flyin' in from Pearl's Place;

Houston-grilled Ribs,
driving over from Harlon's;

Detroit-baked Dressing, who picked up
Macaroni & Cheese from Franklin Street;

& Atlanta, Georgia Peach Cobbler,
who took the midnight train from Q-Time;

Camaraderie rekindles; Life defined—
At the head table I sit...

Giving me the lead to calm Gumbo's
jokes, ask Macaroni to put away her
toys, then bring us home—

& together.

Grandma's soul must be stirring as
her spirit entwines the elements of home
to foster a feast for souls through
this one wonder of the world—

Table set; Corn Bread warmed;
& Grace said—

Where opened eyes span across
the table for generations to connect
and see who inaugurates the meal,
this sphere we know as Earth
reenergizes and begins to turn;

Along our hearts follow toward the
reciprocity of the ancestral souls,
who created & crafted this tool of
unification to always bring us home—
& together;

before dinner is served.

< Interlude: Diagnosis >

i want to believe you somewhere dream
     & rest them subconsciously between the
insomnia you wrestle & the narcolepsy
     you arise to battle—

in a space without border, ceilings,
     margins, or boundaries hearing whispers
that walls needed to come tumbling up—
     to restructure a place reminiscent
of youth, evocative of tranquility
     reminding of home—

to let the misunderstanding & repercussion
     of life echo then dissolve inside a space
between where you've come from & the
     distance you've come to know you must go

you're not alone— case unclosed.

< 100 >

♩140♩

INTRODUCTION TO MUSIC

< by m.a.t. } instruments- Revelations 14:2 >

Your conceivers
exist no more— but

their memories awake
to superior ranks—

through the range
of soundscapes— of

which you appear. In
front of you— i sit

folded legs— eyes closed,
arms down, hands up

toward the heavens— who
accept my praise for

receiving your offering.
You are music— introduced in the

most common & extraordinary
remastering— bringing

peace, connection, &
Love (for you are my

first). You choose not
to believe— but remind

me— i'm no stranger to
hurt— no alien to forgettable

worlds— no unforeseen
diagnosis. Meditating—i inhale

knowing you've shared
secrets— i haven't kept—

unraveled lyrics my bass
focused mind wouldn't

hear— signaled my dawn
awake— which i'd receive— &

fall back asleep. 'Til this
antenna & static free mind

could exhale for your reflection
to rise to superior ranks—

through the range of
soundscapes of

which you appear— not
just in forms of jazz, gospel,

r & b, or hip hop— but in
humanistic rhythms &

poetic tempos from
the music of existence. For

you become human— in full
flesh & soul— here to

show me the way. In front
of you, i stand on

strengthened legs, arms
lifted high— hands expressing

joy to the heavens—
who accept my gratitude

for the common & extraordinary
peace, connection, & Love

you bring. You are music—
introduced & received

in ways that unshackle my
dances— move my spirit—

mediate my soul &
arrange the soundscapes

for me to sing you
your praise.

ACOUSTIC PRAYER

< by m.a.t. } instruments- Ephesians 5:19 >

guitar in hand— music surrounds me

trumpets shout halleluiah;
trombones bellow testimonials;
bass drums dance in spirits;
    while violas string deliverance;

all in perfect harmony

until the piano keys call for silence.

the saxophones rest;
    the flutes un-draw their blinds;
the tambourines bow their heads;

then all woodwind hearts & harmonic minds are cleared.

I sigh in spiritual release from
    a strived-for melodic peace.

guitar in hand— silence surrounding me

    my head can finally bow,
    my watery eyes can now close.

    I feel so moved.

for I've journeyed to study the life art of reading,
composing, & conducting the instruments

    that perform and create distinctive sounds
    I've had to learn to spiritually identify—

without sheets of reference for even the
most foreign echoes of noise.

and my— has my conductibility grown.

I've grown to the clout of piano keys and can silence wrong

oboes in tunes of tribulation;
    cellos on false judgment strings;

even choirs of remorse whispering
        shame in 3-dimensional harmonization;

with just the wave of my hands.

to achieve the most
indescribable & implausible
silence known to man-

a surround silence that awaits
        the commencement of my benediction
alone in unison

with my guitar in hand— to perform the
acoustic prayer.

amen.

ABOUT THE AUTHOR

Born on August 9, 1979, Mark Anthony Thomas has been a literary artist since his teenage years. A member of the Academy of American Poets, Thomas has performed at educational institutions, major civic engagements, and spoken word events, while his works have been championed in literary publications, magazines, newspapers, and on-line. His first book, "As I Look," was released by Amazing Experiences Press in 2000. Thomas, who has been featured in *Atlanta Journal-Constitution*, *Time Magazine*, and on *National Public Radio*, has published more than 200 journalism articles and columns in newspaper and magazine publications. He has been featured by Atlanta's NBC 11-Alive as a "Future Leader of Tomorrow," received an editing award from the Southeastern Journalism Conference, and served on leadership teams for the National Association of Black Journalist's Atlanta affiliate and the Southern Region of Alpha Phi Alpha Fraternity- which named him their "Outstanding Brother of the Year," in 2001. After graduating from the University of Georgia in 2001, he began his professional career in Atlanta, GA as a communications and community programs professional with the Georgia-Pacific Corporation. In 2003, he was selected by the Southeastern Council on Foundations as a Hull Philanthropy Fellow. In 2004, Thomas was elected Chairman of the Board of Directors for Helping Teens Succeed, Inc. At UGA, Thomas became the first African American editor, in the university's bicentennial history, at the independent student newspaper, *The Red & Black*. He is currently active on many non-profit boards and initiatives in the Metro Atlanta community.

"THE POETIC REPERCUSSION" PROJECT SPECIAL THANKS

I have to honor God/Mom/Dad/Bianca/Ernest, Jr/ Grandma Bee/ Uncles/Aunts/Devin/Darius/Tyler/Courtney/Friends of my family/My Life Mentors/Independent Consultants/My GP/Holy Fellowship/Crossroads/ UGA/Redan families/& the many supporters of not only my poetic work, but my life/

To my "Jimmy Jams" and "P-Diddies" during this project-
Tiana/Tanya/Jerrell/Harlan/Gini/ I can't put a value on what your support for me during this project has meant. Diving into an emotional pool to pull words from, can drain even the strongest man. You all have been the great "music of existence"= friends/spiritual guiders/advisors/and just blessings for my life & personal growth. In return- this book is dedicated to you. Thank you & Thank God for you— *Work & Progress.*